CLARENCE

BRET HARTE

Clarence

Bret Harte

© 1st World Library, 2007
PO Box 2211
Fairfield, IA 52556
www.1stworldlibrary.com
First Edition

LCCN: 2007930718

Softcover ISBN: 978-1-4218-4798-6
Hardcover ISBN: 978-1-4218-4701-6
eBook ISBN: 978-1-4218-4895-2

Purchase *"Clarence"*
as a traditional bound book at:
www.1stWorldLibrary.com/purchase.asp?ISBN=978-1-4218-4798-6

1st World Library is a literary, educational organization
dedicated to:

- Creating a free internet library of downloadable ebooks

- Hosting writing competitions and offering book publishing scholarships.

Interested in more 1st World Library books? contact:
literacy@1stworldlibrary.com
Check us out at: www.1stworldlibrary.com

1st World Library Literary Society

Giving Back to the World

"If you want to work on the core problem, it's early school literacy."

- James Barksdale, former CEO of Netscape

"No skill is more crucial to the future of a child, or to a democratic and prosperous society, than literacy."

- Los Angeles Times

"Literacy... means far more than learning how to read and write... The aim is to transmit... knowledge and promote social participation."

- UNESCO

"Literacy is not a luxury, it is a right and a responsibility. If our world is to meet the challenges of the twenty-first century we must harness the energy and creativity of all our citizens."

- President Bill Clinton

"Parents should be encouraged to read to their children, and teachers should be equipped with all available techniques for teaching literacy, so the varying needs and capacities of individual kids can be taken into account."

- Hugh Mackay

PART I

CHAPTER I

As Clarence Brant, President of the Robles Land Company, and husband of the rich widow of John Peyton, of the Robles Ranche, mingled with the outgoing audience of the Cosmopolitan Theatre, at San Francisco, he elicited the usual smiling nods and recognition due to his good looks and good fortune. But as he hurriedly slipped through the still lingering winter's rain into the smart coupe that was awaiting him, and gave the order "Home," the word struck him with a peculiarly ironical significance. His home was a handsome one, and lacked nothing in appointment and comfort, but he had gone to the theatre to evade its hollow loneliness. Nor was it because his wife was not there, for he had a miserable consciousness that her temporary absence had nothing to do with his homelessness. The distraction of the theatre over, that dull, vague, but aching sense of loneliness which was daily growing upon him returned with greater vigor.

He leaned back in the coupe and gloomily reflected.

He had been married scarcely a year, yet even in the illusions of the honeymoon the woman, older than himself, and the widow of his old patron, had half unconsciously reasserted herself, and slipped back into the domination of her old position. It was at first pleasant enough,—this half-maternal protectorate which is apt to mingle even with the affections of younger women,—and Clarence, in his easy, half-feminine intuition of the sex, yielded, as the strong are apt to yield, through the very consciousness of their own superiority. But this is a quality the weaker are not apt to recognize, and the woman who has once tasted equal power with her husband not only does not easily relegate it, but even makes its continuance a test of the affections. The usual triumphant feminine conclusion, "Then you no longer love me," had in Clarence's brief experience gone even further and reached its inscrutable climax, "Then I no longer love you," although shown only in a momentary hardening of the eye and voice. And added to this was his sudden, but confused remembrance that he had seen that eye and heard that voice in marital altercation during Judge Peyton's life, and that he himself, her boy partisan, had sympathized with her. Yet, strange to say, this had given him more pain than her occasional other reversions to the past—to her old suspicious of him when he was a youthful protege of her husband and a presumed suitor of her adopted daughter Susy. High natures are more apt to forgive wrong done to themselves than any abstract injustice. And her capricious tyranny over her dependents and servants, or an unreasoning enmity to a neighbor or friend, outraged his finer sense more than her own misconception of himself. Nor did he dream that this was a thing most women seldom understand, or, understanding, ever forgive.

The coupe rattled over the stones or swirled through the muddy pools of the main thoroughfares. Newspaper and telegraphic offices were still brilliantly lit, and crowds were gathered among the bulletin boards. He knew that news had arrived from Washington that evening of the first active outbreaks of secession, and that the city was breathless with excitement. Had he not just come from the theatre, where

Bret Harte

certain insignificant allusions in the play had been suddenly caught up and cheered or hissed by hitherto unknown partisans, to the dumb astonishment of a majority of the audience comfortably settled to money-getting and their own affairs alone? Had he not applauded, albeit half-scornfully, the pretty actress—his old playmate Susy—who had audaciously and all incongruously waved the American flag in their faces? Yes! he had known it; had lived for the last few weeks in an atmosphere electrically surcharged with it— and yet it had chiefly affected him in his personal homelessness. For his wife was a Southerner, a born slaveholder, and a secessionist, whose noted prejudices to the North had even outrun her late husband's politics. At first the piquancy and recklessness of her opinionative speech amused him as part of her characteristic flavor, or as a lingering youthfulness which the maturer intellect always pardons. He had never taken her politics seriously—why should he? With her head on his shoulder he had listened to her extravagant diatribes against the North. He had forgiven her outrageous indictment of his caste and his associates for the sake of the imperious but handsome lips that uttered it. But when he was compelled to listen to her words echoed and repeated by her friends and family; when he found that with the clannishness of her race she had drawn closer to them in this controversy,—that she depended upon them for her intelligence and information rather than upon him,—he had awakened to the reality of his situation. He had borne the allusions of her brother, whose old scorn for his dependent childhood had been embittered by his sister's marriage and was now scarcely concealed. Yet, while he had never altered his own political faith and social creed in this antagonistic atmosphere, he had often wondered, with his old conscientiousness and characteristic self-abnegation, whether his own political convictions were not merely a revulsion from his domestic tyranny and alien surroundings.

In the midst of this gloomy retrospect the coupe stopped with a jerk before his own house. The door was quickly opened by a servant, who appeared to be awaiting him.

"Some one to see you in the library, sir," said the man, "and"—He hesitated and looked towards the coupe.

"Well?" said Clarence impatiently.

"He said, sir, as how you were not to send away the carriage."

"Indeed, and who is it?" demanded Clarence sharply.

"Mr. Hooker. He said I was to say Jim Hooker."

The momentary annoyance in Clarence's face changed to a look of reflective curiosity.

"He said he knew you were at the theatre, and he would wait until you came home," continued the man, dubiously watching his master's face. "He don't know you've come in, sir, and—and I can easily get rid of him."

"No matter now. I'll see him, and," added Clarence, with a faint smile, "let the carriage wait."

Yet, as he turned towards the library he was by no means certain that an interview with the old associate of his boyhood under Judge Peyton's guardianship would divert his mind. Yet he let no trace of his doubts nor of his past gloom show in his face as he entered the room.

Mr. Hooker was apparently examining the elegant furniture and luxurious accommodation with his usual resentful enviousness. Clarence had got a "soft thing." That it was more or less the result of his "artfulness," and that he was unduly "puffed up" by it, was, in Hooker's characteristic reasoning, equally clear. As his host smilingly advanced with outstretched hand, Mr. Hooker's efforts to assume a proper abstraction of manner and contemptuous indifference to Clarence's surroundings which should wound his vanity ended in his lolling back at full length in the chair with his eyes on the ceiling. But, remembering suddenly that he was really the bearer of a message to Clarence, it struck him that his supine position was, from a theatrical view-point, infelicitous. In his experiences of the stage he had never delivered a message in that way. He rose awkwardly to his feet.

"It was so good of you to wait," said Clarence courteously.

"Saw you in the theatre," said Hooker brusquely. "Third row in parquet. Susy said it was you, and had suthin' to say to you. Suthin' you ought to know," he continued, with a slight return of his old mystery of manner which Clarence so well remembered. "You saw HER—she fetched the house with that flag business, eh? She knows which way the cat is going to jump, you bet. I tell you, for all the blowing of these secessionists, the Union's goin' to pay! Yes, sir!" He stopped, glanced round the handsome room, and added darkly, "Mebbee better than this."

With the memory of Hooker's characteristic fondness for mystery still in his mind, Clarence overlooked the innuendo, and said smilingly,—

"Why didn't you bring Mrs. Hooker here? I should have been honored with her company."

Mr. Hooker frowned slightly at this seeming levity.

"Never goes out after a performance. Nervous exhaustion.

Left her at our rooms in Market Street. We can drive there in ten minutes. That's why I asked to have the carriage wait."

Clarence hesitated. Without caring in the least to renew the acquaintance of his old playmate and sweetheart, a meeting that night in some vague way suggested to him a providential diversion. Nor was he deceived by any gravity in the message. With his remembrance of Susy's theatrical tendencies, he was quite prepared for any capricious futile extravagance.

"You are sure we will not disturb her?" he said politely.

"No."

Clarence led the way to the carriage. If Mr. Hooker expected him during the journey to try to divine the purport of Susy's message he was disappointed. His companion did not allude to it. Possibly looking upon it as a combined theatrical performance, Clarence preferred to wait for Susy as the better actor. The carriage rolled rapidly through the now deserted streets, and at last, under the directions of Mr. Hooker, who was leaning half out of the window, it drew up at a middle-class restaurant, above whose still lit and steaming windows were some ostentatiously public apartments, accessible from a side entrance. As they ascended the staircase together, it became evident that Mr. Hooker was scarcely more at his ease in the character of host than he had been as guest. He stared gloomily at a descending visitor, grunted audibly at a waiter in the passage, and stopped before a door, where a recently deposited tray displayed the half-eaten carcase of a fowl, an empty champagne bottle, two half-filled glasses, and a faded bouquet. The whole passage was redolent with a singular blending of damp cooking, stale cigarette smoke, and patchouli.

Putting the tray aside with his foot, Mr. Hooker opened the door hesitatingly and peered into the room, muttered a few indistinct words, which were followed by a rapid rustling of skirts, and then, with his hand still on the door-knob, turning to Clarence, who had discreetly halted on the threshold, flung the door open theatrically and bade him enter.

"She is somewhere in the suite," he added, with a large wave of the hand towards a door that was still oscillating. "Be here in a minit."

Clarence took in the apartment with a quiet glance. Its furniture had the frayed and discolored splendors of a public parlor which had been privately used and maltreated; there were stains in the large medallioned carpet; the gilded veneer had been chipped from a heavy centre table, showing the rough, white deal beneath, which gave it the appearance of a stage "property;" the walls, paneled with gilt-framed mirrors, reflected every domestic detail or private relaxation with shameless publicity. A damp waterproof, shawl, and open newspaper were lying across the once brilliant sofa; a powder-puff, a plate of fruit, and a play-book were on the centre table, and on the marble-topped sideboard was Mr. Hooker's second-best hat, with a soiled collar, evidently but lately exchanged for the one he had on, peeping over its brim. The whole apartment seemed to mingle the furtive disclosures of the dressing-room with the open ostentations of the stage, with even a slight suggestion of the auditorium in a few scattered programmes on the floor and chairs.

The inner door opened again with a slight theatrical start, and Susy, in an elaborate dressing-gown, moved languidly into the room. She apparently had not had time to change her underskirt, for there was the dust of the stage on its delicate lace edging, as she threw herself into an armchair and crossed her pretty slippered feet before her. Her face was pale, its pallor incautiously increased by powder; and as Clarence looked at its still youthful, charming outline, he was not perhaps sorry that the exquisite pink and white skin beneath, which he had once kissed, was hidden from that awakened recollection. Yet there was little trace of the girlish Susy in the pretty, but prematurely jaded, actress before him, and he felt momentarily relieved. It was her youth and freshness appealing to his own youth and imagination that he had loved—not HER. Yet as she greeted him with a slight exaggeration of glance, voice, and manner, he remembered that even as a girl she was an actress.

Nothing of this, however, was in his voice and manner as he gently thanked her for the opportunity of meeting her again. And he was frank, for the diversion he had expected he had found; he even was conscious of thinking more kindly of his wife who had supplanted her.

"I told Jim he must fetch you if he had to carry you," she said, striking the palm of her hand with her fan, and glancing at her husband. "I reckon he guessed WHY, though I didn't tell him—I don't tell Jim EVERYTHING."

Here Jim rose, and looking at his watch, "guessed he'd run over to the Lick House and get some cigars." If he was acting upon some hint from his wife, his simulation was so badly done that Clarence felt his first sense of uneasiness. But as Hooker closed the door awkwardly and unostentatiously behind him, Clarence smilingly said he had waited to hear the message from her own lips.

"Jim only knows what he's heard outside: the talk of men, you know,—and he hears a good deal of that—more, perhaps, than YOU do. It was that which put me up to finding out the truth. And I didn't rest till I did. I'm not to be fooled, Clarence,—you don't mind my calling you Clarence now we're both married and done for,—and I'm not the kind to be fooled by anybody from the Cow counties—and that's the Robles Ranche. I'm a Southern woman myself from Missouri, but I'm for the Union first, last, and all the time, and I call myself a match for any lazy, dawdling, lash-swinging slaveholder and slaveholderess—whether they're mixed blood, Heaven only knows, or what—or their friends or relations, or the dirty half-Spanish grandees and their mixed half-nigger peons who truckle to them. You bet!"

His blood had stirred quickly at the mention of the Robles Ranche, but the rest of Susy's speech was too much in the vein of her old extravagance to touch him seriously. He found himself only considering how strange it was that the old petulance and impulsiveness of her girlhood were actually bringing back with them her pink cheeks and brilliant eyes.

"You surely didn't ask Jim to bring me here," he said smilingly, "to tell me that Mrs. Peyton"—he corrected himself hastily as a malicious sparkle came into Susy's blue eyes—"that my wife was a Southern woman, and probably sympathized with her class? Well, I don't know that I should blame her for that any more than she should blame me for being a Northern man and a Unionist."

"And she doesn't blame you?" asked Susy sneeringly.

The color came slightly to Clarence's cheek, but before he could reply the actress added,—

"No, she prefers to use you!"

"I don't think I understand you," said Clarence, rising coldly.

"No, you don't understand HER!" retorted Susy sharply.

"Look here, Clarence Brant, you're right; I didn't ask you here to tell you—what you and everybody knows—that your wife is a Southerner. I didn't ask you here to tell you what everybody suspects—that she turns you round her little finger. But I did ask you here to tell you what nobody, not even you, suspects—but what I know!—and that is that she's a TRAITOR—and more, a SPY!—and that I've only got to say the word, or send that man Jim to say the word, to have her dragged out of her Copperhead den at Robles Ranche and shut up in Fort Alcatraz this very night!"

Still with the pink glowing in her rounding cheek, and eyes snapping like splintered sapphires, she rose to her feet, with her pretty shoulders lifted, her small hands and white teeth both tightly clenched, and took a step towards him. Even in her attitude there was a reminiscence of her willful childhood, although still blended with the provincial actress whom he had seen on the stage only an hour ago. Thoroughly alarmed at her threat, in his efforts to conceal his feelings he was not above a weak retaliation. Stepping back, he affected to regard her with a critical admiration that was only half simulated, and said with a smile,—

"Very well done—but you have forgotten the flag."

She did not flinch. Rather accepting the sarcasm as a tribute to her art, she went on with increasing exaggeration: "No, it is YOU who have forgotten the flag—forgotten your country, your people, your manhood—everything for that high-toned, double-dyed old spy and traitress! For while you are standing here, your wife is gathering under her roof at Robles a gang of spies and traitors like herself—secession leaders and their bloated, drunken 'chivalry'! Yes, you may smile your superior smile, but I tell you, Clarence Brant, that with all your smartness and book learning you know no more of what goes on around you than a child. But others do! This conspiracy is known to the government, the Federal officers have been warned; General Sumner has been sent out here—and his first act was to change the command at Fort Alcatraz, and send your wife's Southern friend—Captain Pinckney—to the right about! Yes—everything is known but ONE thing, and that is WHERE and HOW this precious crew meet! That I alone know, and that I've told you!"

"And I suppose," said Clarence, with an unchanged smile, "that this valuable information came from your husband—my old friend, Jim Hooker?"

"No," she answered sharply, "it comes from Cencho—one of your own peons—who is more true to you and the old Rancho than YOU have ever been. He saw what was going on, and came to me, to warn you!"

"But why not to me directly?" asked Clarence, with affected incredulity.

"Ask him!" she said viciously. "Perhaps he didn't want to warn the master against the mistress. Perhaps he thought WE are still friends. Perhaps"—she hesitated with a lower voice and a forced smile—"perhaps he used to see us together in the old times."

"Very likely," said Clarence quietly. "And for the sake of those old times, Susy," he went on, with a singular gentleness that was quite distinct from his paling face and set eyes, "I am going to forget all that you have just said of me and mine, in all the old willfulness and impatience that I see you still keep—with all your old prettiness." He took his hat from the table and gravely held out his hand.

She was frightened for a moment with his impassive abstraction. In the old days she had known it—had believed

it was his dogged "obstinacy"—but she knew the hopeless-
ness of opposing it. Yet with feminine persistency she again
threw herself against it, as against a wall.

"You don't believe me! Well, go and see for yourself. They
are at Robles NOW. If you catch the early morning stage at
Santa Clara you will come upon them before they disperse.
Dare you try it?"

"Whatever I do," he returned smilingly, "I shall always be
grateful to you for giving me this opportunity of seeing you
again AS YOU WERE. Make my excuses to your husband.
Good-night."

"Clarence!"

But he had already closed the door behind him. His face did
not relax its expression nor change as he looked again at the
tray with its broken viands before the door, the worn, stained
hall carpet, or the waiter who shuffled past him. He was
apparently as critically conscious of them and of the close
odors of the hall, and the atmosphere of listless decay and
faded extravagance around him, as before the interview. But
if the woman he had just parted from had watched him she
would have supposed he still utterly disbelieved her story.
Yet he was conscious that all that he saw was a part of his
degradation, for he had believed every word she had uttered.
Through all her extravagance, envy, and revengefulness he
saw the central truth—that he had been deceived—not by his
wife, but by himself! He had suspected all this before. This
was what had been really troubling him—this was what he
had put aside, rather than his faith, not in her, but in his ideal.
He remembered letters that had passed between her and
Captain Pinckney—letters that she had openly sent to
notorious Southern leaders; her nervous anxiety to remain at
the Rancho; the innuendoes and significant glances of

friends which he had put aside—as he had this woman's message! Susy had told him nothing new of his wife—but the truth of HIMSELF! And the revelation came from people who he was conscious were the inferiors of himself and his wife. To an independent, proud, and self-made man it was the culminating stroke.

In the same abstracted voice he told the coachman to drive home. The return seemed interminable—though he never shifted his position. Yet when he drew up at his own door and looked at his watch he found he had been absent only half an hour. Only half an hour! As he entered the house he turned with the same abstraction towards a mirror in the hall, as if he expected to see some outward and visible change in himself in that time. Dismissing his servants to bed, he went into his dressing-room, completely changed his attire, put on a pair of long riding-boots, and throwing a serape over his shoulders, paused a moment, took a pair of small "Derringer" pistols from a box, put them in his pockets, and then slipped cautiously down the staircase. A lack of confidence in his own domestics had invaded him for the first time. The lights were out. He silently opened the door and was in the street.

He walked hastily a few squares to a livery stable whose proprietor he knew. His first inquiry was for one "Redskin," a particular horse; the second for its proprietor. Happily both were in. The proprietor asked no question of a customer of Clarence's condition. The horse, half Spanish, powerful and irascible, was quickly saddled. As Clarence mounted, the man in an impulse of sociability said,—

"Saw you at the theatre to-night, sir."

"Ah," returned Clarence, quietly gathering up the reins.

"Rather a smart trick of that woman with the flag," he went

on tentatively. Then, with a possible doubt of his customer's politics, he added with a forced smile, "I reckon it's all party fuss, though; there ain't any real danger."

But fast as Clarence might ride the words lingered in his ears. He saw through the man's hesitation; he, too, had probably heard that Clarence Brant weakly sympathized with his wife's sentiments, and dared not speak fully. And he understood the cowardly suggestion that there was "no real danger." It had been Clarence's one fallacy. He had believed the public excitement was only a temporary outbreak of partisan feeling, soon to subside. Even now he was conscious that he was less doubtful of the integrity of the Union than of his own household. It was not the devotion of the patriot, but the indignation of an outraged husband, that was spurring him on.

He knew that if he reached Woodville by five o'clock he could get ferried across the bay at the Embarcadero, and catch the down coach to Fair Plains, whence he could ride to the Rancho. As the coach did not connect directly with San Francisco, the chance of his surprising them was greater. Once clear of the city outskirts, he bullied Redskin into irascible speed, and plunged into the rainy darkness of the highroad. The way was familiar. For a while he was content to feel the buffeting, caused by his rapid pace, of wind and rain against his depressed head and shoulders in a sheer brutal sense of opposition and power, or to relieve his pent-up excitement by dashing through overflowed gullies in the road or across the quaggy, sodden edges of meadowland, until he had controlled Redskin's rebellious extravagance into a long steady stride. Then he raised his head and straightened himself on the saddle, to think. But to no purpose. He had no plan; everything would depend upon the situation; the thought of forestalling any action of the conspirators, by warning or calling in the aid of the authorities, for an instant crossed his mind, but was as instantly dismissed. He had but an instinct—to see with his own eyes what his reason told him was true. Day was breaking through drifting scud and pewter-colored clouds as he reached Woodville ferry, checkered with splashes of the soil and the spume of his horse, from whose neck and flanks the sweat rolled like lather. Yet he was not conscious how intent had been his purpose until he felt a sudden instinctive shock on seeing that the ferryboat was gone. For an instant his wonderful self-possession abandoned him; he could only gaze vacantly at the leaden-colored bay, without a thought or expedient. But in another moment he saw that the boat was returning from the distance. Had he lost his only chance? He glanced hurriedly at his watch; he had come more quickly than he imagined; there would still be time. He beckoned impatiently to the ferryman; the boat—a ship's pinnace, with two men in it—crept in with exasperating slowness. At last the two rowers suddenly leaped ashore.

"Ye might have come before, with the other passenger. We don't reckon to run lightnin' trips on this ferry."

But Clarence was himself again. "Twenty dollars for two more oars in that boat," he said quietly, "and fifty if you get me over in time to catch the down stage."

The man glanced at Clarence's eyes. "Run up and rouse out Jake and Sam," he said to the other boatman; then more leisurely, gazing at his customer's travel-stained equipment, he said, "There must have been a heap o' passengers got left by last night's boat. You're the second man that took this route in a hurry."

At any other time the coincidence might have struck Clarence. But he only answered curtly, "Unless we are under way in ten minutes you will find I am NOT the second man, and that our bargain's off."

But here two men emerged from the shanty beside the ferryhouse, and tumbled sleepily into the boat. Clarence seized an extra pair of sculls that were standing against the shed, and threw them into the stern. "I don't mind taking a hand myself for exercise," he said quietly.

The ferryman glanced again at Clarence's travel-worn figure and determined eyes with mingled approval and surprise. He lingered a moment with his oars lifted, looking at his passenger. "It ain't no business o' mine, young man," he said deliberately, "but I reckon you understand me when I say that I've just taken another man over there."

"I do," said Clarence impatiently.

"And you still want to go?"

"Certainly," replied Clarence, with a cold stare, taking up his oars.

The man shrugged his shoulders, bent himself for the stroke, and the boat sprung forward. The others rowed strongly and rapidly, the tough ashen blades springing like steel from the water, the heavy boat seeming to leap in successive bounds until they were fairly beyond the curving inshore current and clearing the placid, misty surface of the bay. Clarence did not speak, but bent abstractedly over his oar; the ferryman and his crew rowed in equal panting silence; a few startled ducks whirred before them, but dropped again to rest. In half an hour they were at the Embarcadero. The time was fairly up. Clarence's eyes were eagerly bent for the first appearance of the stage-coach around the little promontory; the ferryman was as eagerly scanning the bare, empty street of the still sleeping settlement.

Bret Harte

"I don't see him anywhere," said the ferryman with a glance, half of astonishment and half of curiosity, at his solitary passenger.

"See whom?" asked Clarence carelessly, as he handed the man his promised fee.

"The other man I ferried over to catch the stage. He must have gone on without waiting. You're in luck, young fellow!"

"I don't understand you," said Clarence impatiently. "What has your previous passenger to do with me?"

"Well, I reckon you know best. He's the kind of man, gin'rally speaking, that other men, in a pow'ful hurry, don't care to meet—and, az a rule, don't FOLLER arter. It's gin'rally the other way."

"What do you mean?" inquired Clarence sternly. "Of whom are you speaking?"

"The Chief of Police of San Francisco!"

CHAPTER II

The laugh that instinctively broke from Clarence's lips was so sincere and unaffected that the man was disconcerted, and at last joined in it, a little shamefacedly. The grotesque blunder of being taken as a fugitive from justice relieved Clarence's mind from its acute tension,—he was momentarily diverted,—and it was not until the boatman had departed, and he was again alone, that it seemed to have any collateral significance. Then an uneasy recollection of Susy's threat that she had the power to put his wife in Fort Alcatraz came across him. Could she have already warned the municipal authorities and this man? But he quickly remembered that any action from such a warning could only have been taken by the United States Marshal, and not by a civic official, and dismissed the idea.

Nevertheless, when the stage with its half-spent lamps still burning dimly against the morning light swept round the curve and rolled heavily up to the rude shanty which served as coach-office, he became watchful. A single yawning individual in its doorway received a few letters and parcels, but Clarence was evidently the ONLY waiting passenger. Any hope that he might have entertained that his mysterious predecessor would emerge from some seclusion at that moment was disappointed. As he entered the coach he made a rapid survey of his fellow-travelers, but satisfied himself

Bret Harte

that the stranger was not among them. They were mainly small traders or farmers, a miner or two, and apparently a Spanish-American of better degree and personality. Possibly the circumstance that men of this class usually preferred to travel on horseback and were rarely seen in public conveyances attracted his attention, and their eyes met more than once in mutual curiosity. Presently Clarence addressed a remark to the stranger in Spanish; he replied fluently and courteously, but at the next stopping-place he asked a question of the expressman in an unmistakable Missouri accent. Clarence's curiosity was satisfied; he was evidently one of those early American settlers who had been so long domiciled in Southern California as to adopt the speech as well as the habiliments of the Spaniard.

The conversation fell upon the political news of the previous night, or rather seemed to be lazily continued from some previous, more excited discussion, in which one of the contestants—a red-bearded miner—had subsided into an occasional growl of surly dissent. It struck Clarence that the Missourian had been an amused auditor and even, judging from a twinkle in his eye, a mischievous instigator of the controversy. He was not surprised, therefore, when the man turned to him with a certain courtesy and said,—

"And what, sir, is the political feeling in YOUR district?"

But Clarence was in no mood to be drawn out, and replied, almost curtly, that as he had come only from San Francisco, they were probably as well informed on that subject as himself. A quick and searching glance from the stranger's eye made him regret his answer, but in the silence that ensued the red-bearded miner, evidently still rankling at heart, saw his opportunity. Slapping his huge hands on his knees, and leaning far forward until he seemed to plunge his flaming beard, like a firebrand, into the controversy, he said grimly,—

"Well, I kin tell you, gen'l'men, THIS. It ain't goin' to be no matter wot's the POLITICAL FEELING here or thar—it ain't goin' to be no matter wot's the State's rights and wot's Fed'ral rights—it ain't goin' to be no question whether the gov'ment's got the right to relieve its own soldiers that those Secesh is besieging in Fort Sumter or whether they haven't—but the first gun that's fired at the flag blows the chains off every d—n nigger south of Mason and Dixon's line! You hear me! I'm shoutin'! And whether you call yourselves 'Secesh' or 'Union' or 'Copperhead' or 'Peace men,' you've got to face it!"

There was an angry start in one or two of the seats; one man caught at the swinging side-strap and half rose, a husky voice began, "It's a d—d"—and then all as suddenly subsided. Every eye was turned to an insignificant figure in the back seat. It was a woman, holding a child on her lap, and gazing out of the window with her sex's profound unconcern in politics. Clarence understood the rude chivalry of the road well enough to comprehend that this unconscious but omnipotent figure had more than once that day controlled the passions of the disputants. They dropped back weakly to their seats, and their mutterings rolled off in the rattle of the wheels. Clarence glanced at the Missourian; he was regarding the red-bearded miner with a singular curiosity.

The rain had ceased, but the afternoon shadows were deepening when they at last reached Fair Plains, where Clarence expected to take horse to the Rancho. He was astonished, however, to learn that all the horses in the stable were engaged, but remembering that some of his own stock were in pasturage with a tenant at Fair Plains, and that he should probably have a better selection, he turned his steps thither. Passing out of the stable-yard he recognized the Missourian's voice in whispered conversation with the proprietor, but the two men withdrew into the shadow as he approached. An ill-defined uneasiness came over him; he

Bret Harte

knew the proprietor, who also seemed to know the Missourian, and this evident avoidance of him was significant. Perhaps his reputation as a doubtful Unionist had preceded him, but this would not account for their conduct in a district so strongly Southern in sympathy as Fair Plains. More impressed by the occurrence than he cared to admit, when at last, after some delay, he had secured his horse, and was once more in the saddle, he kept a sharp lookout for his quondam companion. But here another circumstance added to his suspicions: there was a main road leading to Santa Inez, the next town, and the Rancho, and this Clarence had purposely taken in order to watch the Missourian; but there was also a cutoff directly to the Rancho, known only to the habitues of the Rancho. After a few moments' rapid riding on a mustang much superior to any in the hotel stables, he was satisfied that the stranger must have taken the cut-off. Putting spurs to his horse he trusted still to precede him to the Rancho—if that were his destination.

As he dashed along the familiar road, by a strange perversity of fancy, instead of thinking of his purpose, he found himself recalling the first time he had ridden that way in the flush of his youth and hopefulness. The girl-sweetheart he was then going to rejoin was now the wife of another; the woman who had been her guardian was now his own wife. He had accepted without a pang the young girl's dereliction, but it was through her revelation that he was now about to confront the dereliction of his own wife. And this was the reward of his youthful trust and loyalty! A bitter laugh broke from his lips. It was part of his still youthful self-delusion that he believed himself wiser and stronger for it.

It was quite dark when he reached the upper field or first terrace of the Rancho. He could see the white walls of the casa rising dimly out of the green sea of early wild grasses, like a phantom island. It was here that the cut-off joined the main road—now the only one that led to the casa. He was satisfied that no one could have preceded him from Fair Plains; but it was true that he must take precautions against his own discovery. Dismounting near a clump of willows, he unsaddled and unbridled his horse, and with a cut of the riata over its haunches sent it flying across the field in the direction of a band of feeding mustangs, which it presently joined. Then, keeping well in the shadow of a belt of shrub-oaks, he skirted the long lesser terraces of the casa, intending to approach the house by way of the old garden and corral. A drizzling rain, occasionally driven by the wind into long, misty, curtain-like waves, obscured the prospect and favored his design. He reached the low adobe wall of the corral in safety; looking over he could detect, in spite of the darkness, that a number of the horses were of alien brands, and even recognized one or two from the Santa Inez district. The vague outline of buggies and carryalls filled the long shed beside the stables. There WAS company at the casa—so far Susy was right!

Nevertheless, lingering still by the wall of the old garden for the deepening of night, his nervous feverishness was again invaded and benumbed by sullen memories. There was the opening left by the old grille in the wall, behind which Mrs. Peyton stood on the morning when he thought he was leaving the ranch forever; where he had first clasped her in his arms, and stayed. A turn of the head, a moment's indecision, a single glance of a languorous eye, had brought this culmination. And now he stood again before that ruined grille, his house and lands, even his NAME, misused by a mad, scheming enthusiast, and himself a creeping spy of his own dishonor! He turned with a bitter smile again to the garden. A few dark red Castilian roses still leaned forward and swayed in the wind with dripping leaves. It was here that the first morning of his arrival he had kissed Susy; the perfume and color of her pink skin came back to him with a

Bret Harte

sudden shock as he stood there; he caught at a flower, drew it towards him, inhaled its odor in a long breath that left him faint and leaning against the wall. Then again he smiled, but this time more wickedly—in what he believed his cynicism had sprung up the first instinct of revenge!

It was now dark enough for him to venture across the carriage road and make his way to the rear of the house. His first characteristic instinct had been to enter openly at his own front gate, but the terrible temptation to overhear and watch the conspiracy unobserved—that fascination common to deceived humanity to witness its own shame—had now grown upon him. He knew that a word or gesture of explanation, apology, appeal, or even terror from his wife would check his rage and weaken his purpose. His perfect knowledge of the house and the security of its inmates would enable him from some obscure landing or gallery to participate in any secret conclave they might hold in the patio—the only place suitable for so numerous a rendezvous. The absence of light in the few external windows pointed to this central gathering. And he had already conceived his plan of entrance.

Gaining the rear wall of the casa he began cautiously to skirt its brambly base until he had reached a long, oven-like window half obliterated by a monstrous passion vine. It was the window of what had once been Mrs. Peyton's boudoir; the window by which he had once forced an entrance to the house when it was in the hands of squatters, the window from which Susy had signaled her Spanish lover, the window whose grating had broken the neck of Judge Peyton's presumed assassin. But these recollections no longer delayed him; the moment for action had arrived. He knew that since the tragedy the boudoir had been dismantled and shunned; the servants believed it to be haunted by the assassin's ghost. With the aid of the passion vine the ingress was easy; the interior window was open; the rustle of dead leaves on the bare floor as he entered, and the whir of a frightened bird by his ear, told the story of its desolation and the source of the strange noises that had been heard there. The door leading to the corridor was lightly bolted, merely to keep it from rattling in the wind. Slipping the bolt with the blade of his pocket-knife he peered into the dark passage. The light streaming under a door to the left, and the sound of voices, convinced him that his conjecture was right, and the meeting was gathered on the broad balconies around the patio. He knew that a narrow gallery, faced with Venetian blinds to exclude the sun, looked down upon them. He managed to gain it without discovery; luckily the blinds were still down; between their slats, himself invisible, he could hear and see everything that occurred.

Yet even at this supreme moment the first thing that struck him was the almost ludicrous contrast between the appearance of the meeting and its tremendous object. Whether he was influenced by any previous boyish conception of a clouded and gloomy conspiracy he did not know, but he was for an instant almost disconcerted by the apparent levity and festivity of the conclave. Decanters and glasses stood on small tables before them; nearly all were drinking and smoking. They comprised fifteen or twenty men, some of whose faces were familiar to him elsewhere as Southern politicians; a few, he was shocked to see, were well-known Northern Democrats. Occupying a characteristically central position was the famous Colonel Starbottle, of Virginia. Jaunty and youthful-looking in his mask-like, beardless face, expansive and dignified in his middle-aged port and carriage, he alone retained some of the importance—albeit slightly theatrical and affected—of the occasion. Clarence in his first hurried glance had not observed his wife, and for a moment had felt relieved; but as Colonel Starbottle arose at that moment, and with a studiously chivalrous and courtly manner turned to his right, he saw that she was sitting at the further end of the balcony, and that a man whom he recognized as Captain Pinckney was standing beside her. The blood quickly tightened around his heart, but left him cold and observant.

"It was seldom, indeed," remarked Colonel Starbottle, placing his fat fingers in the frill of his shirt front, "that a movement like this was graced with the actual presence of a lofty, inspiring, yet delicate spirit—a Boadicea—indeed, he might say a Joan of Arc—in the person of their charming hostess, Mrs. Brant. Not only were they favored by her social and hospitable ministration, but by her active and enthusiastic cooperation in the glorious work they had in hand. It was through her correspondence and earnest advocacy that they were to be favored to-night with the aid and counsel of one of the most distinguished and powerful men in the Southern district of California, Judge Beeswinger, of Los Angeles. He had not the honor of that gentleman's personal acquaintance; he believed he was not far wrong in saying that this was also the misfortune of every gentleman present; but the name itself was a tower of strength. He would go further, and say that Mrs. Brant herself was personally unacquainted with him, but it was through the fervor, poetry, grace, and genius of her correspondence with that gentleman that they were to have the honor of his presence that very evening. It was understood that advices had been received of his departure, and that he might be expected at Robles at any moment."

"But what proof have we of Judge Beeswinger's soundness?" said a lazy Southern voice at the conclusion of Colonel Starbottle's periods. "Nobody here seems to know him by sight: is it not risky to admit a man to our meeting whom we are unable to identify?"

"I reckon nobody but a fool or some prying mudsill of a Yankee would trust his skin here," returned another; "and if he did we'd know what to do with him."

But Clarence's attention was riveted on his wife, and the significant speech passed him as unheeded as had the colonel's rhetoric. She was looking very handsome and slightly flushed, with a proud light in her eyes that he had never seen before. Absorbed in the discussion, she seemed to be paying little attention to Captain Pinckney as she rose suddenly to her feet.

"Judge Beeswinger will be attended here by Mr. MacNiel, of the Fair Plains Hotel, who will vouch for him and introduce him," she said in a clear voice, which rang with an imperiousness that Clarence well remembered. "The judge was to arrive by the coach from Martinez to Fair Plains, and is due now."

"Is there no GENTLEMAN to introduce him? Must we take him on the word of a common trader—by Jove! a whiskey-seller?" continued the previous voice sneeringly.

"On the word of a lady, Mr. Brooks," said Captain Pinckney, with a slight gesture towards Mrs. Brant—"who answers for both."

Clarence had started slightly at his wife's voice and the information it conveyed. His fellow-passenger, and the confidant of MacNiel, was the man they were expecting! If they had recognized him, Clarence, would they not warn the company of his proximity? He held his breath as the sound of voices came from the outer gate of the courtyard. Mrs. Brant rose; at the same moment the gate swung open, and a man entered. It WAS the Missourian.

He turned with old-fashioned courtesy to the single woman standing on the balcony.

"My fair correspondent, I believe! I am Judge Beeswinger. Your agent, MacNiel, passed me through your guards at the gate, but I did not deem it advisable to bring him into this assembly of gentlemen without your further consideration. I trust I was right."

The quiet dignity and self-possession, the quaint, old-fashioned colonial precision of speech, modified by a soft Virginian intonation, and, above all, some singular individuality of the man himself, produced a profound sensation, and seemed to suddenly give the gathering an impressiveness it had lacked before. For an instant Clarence forgot himself and his personal wrongs in the shock of indignation he felt at this potent addition to the ranks of his enemies. He saw his wife's eyes sparkle with pride over her acquisition, and noticed that Pinckney cast a disturbed glance at the newcomer.

The stranger ascended the few steps to the balcony and took Mrs. Brant's hand with profound courtesy. "Introduce me to my colleagues—distinctly and separately. It behooves a man at such a moment to know to whom he entrusts his life and honor, and the life and honor of his cause."

It was evidently no mere formal courtesy to the stranger. As he stepped forward along the balcony, and under Mrs. Brant's graceful guidance was introduced to each of the members, he not only listened with scrupulous care and attention to the name and profession of each man, but bent upon him a clear, searching glance that seemed to photograph him in his memory. With two exceptions. He passed Colonel Starbottle's expanding shirt frill with a bow of elaborate precision, and said, "Colonel Starbottle's fame requires neither introduction nor explanation." He stopped before Captain Pinckney and paused.

"An officer of the United States army, I believe, sir?"

"Yes."

"Educated at West Point, I think, by the government, to whom you have taken the oath of allegiance?"

"Yes."

"Very good, sir," said the stranger, turning away.

"You have forgotten one other fact, sir," said Pinckney, with a slightly supercilious air.

"Indeed! What is it?"

"I am, first of all, a native of the State of South Carolina!"

A murmur of applause and approval ran round the balcony. Captain Pinckney smiled and exchanged glances with Mrs. Brant, but the stranger quietly returned to the central table beside Colonel Starbottle. "I am not only an unexpected delegate to this august assembly, gentlemen," he began gravely, "but I am the bearer of perhaps equally unexpected news. By my position in the Southern district I am in possession of dispatches received only this morning by pony express. Fort Sumter has been besieged. The United States flag, carrying relief to the beleaguered garrison, has been fired upon by the State of South Carolina."

A burst of almost hysteric applause and enthusiasm broke from the assembly, and made the dim, vault-like passages and corridors of the casa ring. Cheer after cheer went up to the veiled gallery and the misty sky beyond. Men mounted on the tables and waved their hands frantically, and in the midst of this bewildering turbulence of sound and motion Clarence saw his wife mounted on a chair, with burning cheeks and flashing eyes, waving her handkerchief like an inspired priestess. Only the stranger, still standing beside Colonel Starbottle, remained unmoved and impassive. Then, with an imperative gesture, he demanded a sudden silence.

"Convincing and unanimous as this demonstration is, gentlemen," he began quietly, "it is my duty, nevertheless, to ask you if you have seriously considered the meaning of the news I have brought. It is my duty to tell you that it means civil war. It means the clash of arms between two sections of a mighty country; it means the disruption of friends, the breaking of family ties, the separation of fathers and sons, of brothers and sisters—even, perhaps, to the disseverment of husband and wife!"

"It means the sovereignty of the South—and the breaking of a covenant with lowborn traders and abolitionists," said Captain Pinckney.

"If there are any gentlemen present," continued the stranger, without heeding the interruption, "who have pledged this State to the support of the South in this emergency, or to the establishment of a Pacific republic in aid and sympathy with it, whose names are on this paper"—he lifted a sheet of paper lying before Colonel Starbottle—"but who now feel that the gravity of the news demands a more serious consideration of the purpose, they are at liberty to withdraw from the meeting, giving their honor, as Southern gentlemen, to keep the secret intact."

"Not if I know it," interrupted a stalwart Kentuckian, as he rose to his feet and strode down the steps to the patio. "For," he added, placing his back against the gateway, "I'll shoot the first coward that backs out now."

A roar of laughter and approval followed, but was silenced again by the quiet, unimpassioned voice of the stranger. "If, on the other hand," he went on calmly, "you all feel that this news is the fitting culmination and consecration of the hopes, wishes, and plans of this meeting, you will assert it again, over your own signatures, to Colonel Starbottle at this table."

When the Kentuckian had risen, Clarence had started from his concealment; when he now saw the eager figures pressing forward to the table he hesitated no longer. Slipping along the passage, he reached the staircase which led to the corridor in the rear of the balcony. Descending this rapidly, he not only came upon the backs of the excited crowd around the table, but even elbowed one of the conspirators aside without being noticed. His wife, who had risen from her chair at the end of the balcony, was already moving towards the table. With a quick movement he seized her wrist, and threw her back in the chair again. A cry broke from her lips as she recognized him, but still holding her wrist, he stepped quickly between her and the astonished crowd. There was a moment of silence, then the cry of "Spy!" and "Seize him!" rose quickly, but above all the voice and figure of the Missourian was heard commanding them to stand back. Turning to Clarence, he said quietly,—

"I should know your face, sir. Who are you?"

"The husband of this woman and the master of this house," said Clarence as quietly, but in a voice he hardly recognized as his own.

"Stand aside from her, then—unless you are hoping that her danger may protect YOU!" said the Kentuckian, significantly

Bret Harte

drawing his revolver.

But Mrs. Brant sprang suddenly to her feet beside Clarence.

"We are neither of us cowards, Mr. Brooks—though he speaks the truth—and—more shame to me"—she added, with a look of savage scorn at Clarence—"IS MY HUSBAND!"

"What is your purpose in coming here?" continued Judge Beeswinger, with his eyes fixed on Clarence.

"I have given you all the information," said Clarence quietly, "that is necessary to make you, as a gentleman, leave this house at once—and that is my purpose. It is all the information you will get from me as long as you and your friends insult my roof with your uninvited presence. What I may have to say to you and each of you hereafter—what I may choose to demand of you, according to your own code of honor,"—he fixed his eyes on Captain Pinckney's,—"is another question, and one not usually discussed before a lady."

"Pardon me. A moment—a single moment."

It was the voice of Colonel Starbottle; it was the frilled shirt front, the lightly buttoned blue coat with its expanding lapels, like bursting petals, and the smiling mask of that gentleman rising above the table and bowing to Clarence Brant and his wife with infinite courtesy. "The—er—humiliating situation in which we find ourselves, gentlemen,—the reluctant witnesses of—er—what we trust is only a temporary disagreement between our charming hostess and the—er—gentleman whom she recognized under the highest title to our consideration,—is distressing to us all, and would seem to amply justify that gentleman's claims to a personal satisfaction, which I know we would all delight to give. But that situation rests upon the supposition that our gathering here was of a purely social or festive nature! It may be," continued the colonel with a blandly reflective air, "that the spectacle of these decanters and glasses, and the nectar furnished us by our Hebe-like hostess" (he lifted a glass of whiskey and water to his lips while he bowed to Mrs. Brant gracefully), "has led the gentleman to such a deduction. But when I suggest to him that our meeting was of a business, or private nature, it strikes me that the question of intrusion may be fairly divided between him and ourselves. We may be even justified, in view of that privacy, in asking him if his—er—entrance to this house was—er—coincident with his appearance among us."

"With my front door in possession of strangers," said Clarence, more in reply to a sudden contemptuous glance from his wife than Starbottle's insinuation, "I entered the house through the window."

"Of my boudoir, where another intruder once broke his neck," interrupted his wife with a mocking laugh.

"Where I once helped this lady to regain possession of her house when it was held by another party of illegal trespassers, who, however, were content to call themselves 'jumpers,' and did not claim the privacy of gentlemen."

"Do you mean to imply, sir," began Colonel Starbottle haughtily, "that"—

"I mean to imply, sir," said Clarence with quiet scorn, "that I have neither the wish to know nor the slightest concern in any purpose that brought you here, and that when you quit the house you take your secrets and your privacy with you intact, without let or hindrance from me."

"Do you mean to say, Mr. Brant," said Judge Beeswinger, suppressing the angry interruption of his fellows with a dominant wave of his hand, as he fixed his eyes on Clarence keenly, "that you have no sympathy with your wife's political sentiments?"

"I have already given you the information necessary to make you quit this house, and that is all you have a right to know," returned Clarence with folded arms.

"But I can answer for him," said Mrs. Brant, rising, with a quivering voice and curling lip. "There IS no sympathy between us. We are as far apart as the poles. We have nothing in common but this house and his name."

"But you are husband and wife, bound together by a sacred compact."

"A compact!" echoed Mrs. Brant, with a bitter laugh. "Yes, the compact that binds South Carolina to the nigger-worshipping Massachusetts. The compact that links together white and black, the gentleman and the trader, the planter and the poor white—the compact of those UNITED States. Bah! THAT has been broken, and so can this."

Clarence's face paled. But before he could speak there was a rapid clattering at the gate and a dismounted vaquero entered excitedly. Turning to Mrs. Brant he said hurriedly, "Mother of God! the casa is surrounded by a rabble of mounted men, and there is one among them even now who demands admittance in the name of the Law."

"This is your work," said Brooks, facing Clarence furiously. "You have brought them with you, but, by God, they shall not save you!" He would have clutched Clarence, but the powerful arm of Judge Beeswinger intervened. Nevertheless, he still struggled to reach Clarence, appealing to the others: "Are you fools to stand there and let him triumph! Don't you see the cowardly Yankee trick he's played upon us?"

"He has not," said Mrs. Brant haughtily. "I have no reason to love him or his friends; but I know he does not lie."

"Gentlemen!—gentlemen!" implored Colonel Starbottle with beaming and unctuous persuasion, "may I—er—remark—that all this is far from the question? Are we to be alarmed because an unknown rabble, no matter whence they come, demand entrance here in the name of the Law? I am not aware of any law of the State of California that we are infringing. By all means admit them."

The gate was thrown open. A single thick-set man, apparently unarmed and dressed like an ordinary traveler, followed by half a dozen other equally unpretentious-looking men, entered. The leader turned to the balcony.

"I am the Chief of Police of San Francisco. I have warrants for the arrest of Colonel Culpepper Starbottle, Joshua Brooks, Captain Pinckney, Clarence Brant and Alice his wife, and others charged with inciting to riot and unlawful practice calculated to disturb the peace of the State of California and its relations with the Federal government," said the leader, in a dry official voice.

Clarence started. In spite of its monotonous utterance it was the voice of the red-bearded controversialist of the stage-coach. But where were his characteristic beard and hair? Involuntarily Clarence glanced at Judge Beeswinger; that gentleman was quietly regarding the stranger with an impassive face that betrayed no recognition whatever.

"But the city of San Francisco has no jurisdiction here," said

Colonel Starbottle, turning a bland smile towards his fellow-members. "I am—er—sorry to inform you that you are simply trespassing, sir."

"I am here also as deputy sheriff," returned the stranger coolly. "We were unable to locate the precise place of this meeting, although we knew of its existence. I was sworn in this morning at Santa Inez by the judge of this district, and these gentlemen with me are my posse."

There was a quick movement of resistance by the members, which was, however, again waived blandly aside by Colonel Starbottle. Leaning forward in a slightly forensic attitude, with his fingers on the table and a shirt frill that seemed to have become of itself erectile, he said, with pained but polite precision, "I grieve to have to state, sir, that even that position is utterly untenable here. I am a lawyer myself, as my friend here, Judge Beeswinger—eh? I beg your pardon!"

The officer of the law had momentarily started, with his eyes fixed on Judge Beeswinger, who, however, seemed to be quietly writing at the table.

"As Judge Beeswinger," continued Colonel Starbottle, "will probably tell you and as a jurist himself, he will also probably agree with me when I also inform you that, as the United States government is an aggrieved party, it is a matter for the Federal courts to prosecute, and that the only officer we can recognize is the United States Marshal for the district. When I add that the marshal, Colonel Crackenthorpe, is one of my oldest friends, and an active sympathizer with the South in the present struggle, you will understand that any action from him in this matter is exceedingly improbable."

The general murmur of laughter, relief, and approval was

broken by the quiet voice of Judge Beeswinger.

"Let me see your warrant, Mr. Deputy Sheriff."

The officer approached him with a slightly perplexed and constrained air, and exhibited the paper. Judge Beeswinger handed it back to him. "Colonel Starbottle is quite right in his contention," he said quietly; "the only officer that this assembly can recognize is the United States Marshal or his legal deputy. But Colonel Starbottle is wrong in his supposition that Colonel Crackenthorpe still retains the functions of that office. He was removed by the President of the United States, and his successor was appointed and sworn in by the Federal judge early this morning." He paused, and folding up the paper on which he had been writing, placed it in the hands of the deputy. "And this," he continued in the same even voice, "constitutes you his deputy, and will enable you to carry out your duty in coming here."

"What the devil does this mean, sir? Who are you?" gasped Colonel Starbottle, recoiling suddenly from the man at his side.

"I am the new United States Marshal for the Southern District of California."

CHAPTER III

Unsuspected and astounding as the revelation was to Clarence, its strange reception by the conspirators seemed to him as astounding. He had started forward, half expecting that the complacent and self-confessed spy would be immolated by his infuriated dupes. But to his surprise the shock seemed to have changed their natures, and given them the dignity they had lacked. The excitability, irritation, and recklessness which had previously characterized them had disappeared. The deputy and his posse, who had advanced to the assistance of their revealed chief, met with no resistance. They had evidently, as if with one accord, drawn away from Judge Beeswinger, leaving a cleared space around him, and regarded their captors with sullen contemptuous silence. It was only broken by Colonel Starbottle:—

"Your duty commands you, sir, to use all possible diligence in bringing us before the Federal judge of this district— unless your master in Washington has violated the Constitution so far as to remove him, too!"

"I understand you perfectly," returned Judge Beeswinger, with unchanged composure; "and as you know that Judge Wilson unfortunately cannot be removed except through a regular course of impeachment, I suppose you may still count upon his Southern sympathies to befriend you. With that I have nothing to do; my duty is complete when my deputy has brought you before him and I have stated the circumstances of the arrest."

"I congratulate you, sir," said Captain Pinckney, with an ironical salute, "on your prompt reward for your treachery to the South, and your equally prompt adoption of the peculiar tactics of your friends in the way in which you have entered this house."

"I am sorry I cannot congratulate YOU, sir," returned Judge Beeswinger gravely, "on breaking your oath to the government which has educated and supported you and given you the epaulettes you disgrace. Nor shall I discuss 'treachery' with the man who has not only violated the trust of his country, but even the integrity of his friend's household. It is for that reason that I withhold the action of this warrant in so far as it affects the persons of the master and mistress of this home. I am satisfied that Mr. Brant has been as ignorant of what has been done here as I am that his wife has been only the foolish dupe of a double traitor!"

"Silence!"

The words broke simultaneously from the lips of Clarence and Captain Pinckney. They stood staring at each other—the one pale, the other crimson—as Mrs. Brant, apparently oblivious of the significance of their united adjuration, turned to Judge Beeswinger in the fury of her still stifled rage and mortification.

"Keep your mercy for your fellow-spy," she said, with a contemptuous gesture towards her husband; "I go with these gentlemen!"

"You will not," said Clarence quietly, "until I have said a

Bret Harte

word to you alone." He laid his hand firmly upon her wrist.

The deputy and his prisoners filed slowly out of the courtyard together, the latter courteously saluting Mrs. Brant as they passed, but turning from Judge Beeswinger in contemptuous silence. The judge followed them to the gate, but there he paused. Turning to Mrs. Brant, who was still half struggling in the strong grip of her husband, he said,—

"Any compunction I may have had in misleading you by accepting your invitation here I dismissed after I had entered this house. And I trust," he added, turning to Clarence sternly, "I leave you the master of it!"

As the gate closed behind him, Clarence locked it. When his wife turned upon him angrily, he said quietly,—

"I have no intention of restraining your liberty a moment after our interview is over, but until then I do not intend to be disturbed."

She threw herself disdainfully back in her chair, her hands clasped in her lap in half-contemptuous resignation, with her eyes upon her long slim arched feet crossed before her. Even in her attitude there was something of her old fascination which, however, now seemed to sting Clarence to the quick.

"I have nothing to say to you in regard to what has just passed in this house, except that as long as I remain even nominally its master it shall not be repeated. Although I shall no longer attempt to influence or control your political sympathies, I shall not allow you to indulge them where in any way they seem to imply my sanction. But so little do I oppose your liberty, that you are free to rejoin your political companions whenever you choose to do so on your own responsibility. But I must first know from your own lips whether your sympathies are purely political—or a name for something else?"

She had alternately flushed and paled, although still keeping her scornful attitude as he went on, but there was no mistaking the genuineness of her vague wonderment at his concluding words.

"I don't understand you," she said, lifting her eyes to his in a moment of cold curiosity. "What do you mean?"

"What do I mean? What did Judge Beeswinger mean when he called Captain Pinckney a double traitor?" he said roughly.

She sprang to her feet with flashing eyes. "And you—YOU! dare to repeat the cowardly lie of a confessed spy. This, then, is what you wished to tell me—this the insult for which you have kept me here; because you are incapable of understanding unselfish patriotism or devotion—even to your own cause—you dare to judge me by your own base, Yankee-trading standards. Yes, it is worthy of you!" She walked rapidly up and down, and then suddenly faced him. "I understand it all; I appreciate your magnanimity now. You are willing I should join the company of these chivalrous gentlemen in order to give color to your calumnies! Say at once that it was you who put up this spy to correspond with me—to come here—in order to entrap me. Yes entrap me— I—who a moment ago stood up for you before these gentlemen, and said you could not lie. Bah!"

Struck only by the wild extravagance of her speech and temper, Clarence did not know that when women are most illogical they are apt to be most sincere, and from a man's standpoint her unreasoning deductions appeared to him only as an affectation to gain time for thought, or a theatrical display, like Susy's. And he was turning half contemptuously away, when she again faced him with flashing eyes.

"Well, hear me! I accept; I leave here at once, to join my own people, my own friends—those who understand me—put what construction on it that you choose. Do your worst; you cannot do more to separate us than you have done just now."

She left him, and ran up the steps with a singular return of her old occasional nymph-like nimbleness—the movement of a woman who had never borne children—and a swish of her long skirts that he remembered for many a day after, as she disappeared in the corridor. He remained looking after her—indignant, outraged, and unconvinced. There was a rattling at the gate.

He remembered he had locked it. He opened it to the flushed pink cheeks and dancing eyes of Susy. The rain was still dripping from her wet cloak as she swung it from her shoulders.

"I know it all!—all that's happened," she burst out with half-girlish exuberance and half the actress's declamation. "We met them all in the road—posse and prisoners. Chief Thompson knew me and told me all. And so you've done it—and you're master in your old house again. Clarence, old boy! Jim said you wouldn't do it—said you'd weaken on account of her! But I said 'No.' I knew you better, old Clarence, and I saw it in your face, for all your stiffness! ha! But for all that I was mighty nervous and uneasy, and I just made Jim send an excuse to the theatre and we rushed it down here! Lordy! but it looks natural to see the old house again! And she—you packed her off with the others—didn't you? Tell me, Clarence," in her old appealing voice, "you shook her, too!"

Dazed and astounded, and yet experiencing a vague sense of relief with something like his old tenderness towards the willful woman before him, he had silently regarded her until her allusion to his wife recalled him to himself.

"Hush!" he said quickly, with a glance towards the corridor.

"Ah!" said Susy, with a malicious smile, "then that's why Captain Pinckney was lingering in the rear with the deputy."

"Silence!" repeated Clarence sternly. "Go in there," pointing to the garden room below the balcony, "and wait there with your husband."

He half led, half pushed her into the room which had been his business office, and returned to the patio. A hesitating voice from the balcony said, "Clarence!"

It was his wife's voice, but modified and gentler—more like her voice as he had first heard it, or as if it had been chastened by some reminiscence of those days. It was his wife's face, too, that looked down on his—paler than he had seen it since he entered the house. She was shawled and hooded, carrying a traveling-bag in her hand.

"I am going, Clarence," she said, pausing before him, with gentle gravity, "but not in anger. I even ask you to forgive me for the foolish words that I think your still more foolish accusation"—she smiled faintly—"dragged from me. I am going because I know that I have brought—and that while I am here I shall always be bringing—upon you the imputation and even the responsibility of my own faith! While I am proud to own it,—and if needs be suffer for it,—I have no right to ruin your prospects, or even make you the victim of the slurs that others may cast upon me. Let us part as friends— separated only by our different political faiths, but keeping all other faiths together—until God shall settle the right of this struggle. Perhaps it may be soon—I sometimes think it may be years of agony for all; but until then, good-by."

She had slowly descended the steps to the patio, looking handsomer than he had ever seen her, and as if sustained and upheld by the enthusiasm of her cause. Her hand was outstretched towards his—his heart beat violently—in another moment he might have forgotten all and clasped her to his breast. Suddenly she stopped, her outstretched arm stiffened, her finger pointed to the chair on which Susy's cloak was hanging.

"What's that?" she said in a sharp, high, metallic voice. "Who is here? Speak!"

"Susy," said Clarence.

She cast a scathing glance round the patio, and then settled her piercing eyes on Clarence with a bitter smile.

"Already!"

Clarence felt the blood rush to his face as he stammered, "She knew what was happening here, and came to give you warning."

"Liar!"

"Stop!" said Clarence, with a white face. "She came to tell me that Captain Pinckney was still lingering for you in the road."

He threw open the gate to let her pass. As she swept out she lifted her hand. As he closed the gate there were the white marks of her four fingers on his cheek.

CHAPTER IV

For once Susy had not exaggerated. Captain Pinckney WAS lingering, with the deputy who had charge of him, on the trail near the casa. It had already been pretty well understood by both captives and captors that the arrest was simply a legal demonstration; that the sympathizing Federal judge would undoubtedly order the discharge of the prisoners on their own recognizances, and it was probable that the deputy saw no harm in granting Pinckney's request—which was virtually only a delay in his liberation. It was also possible that Pinckney had worked upon the chivalrous sympathies of the man by professing his disinclination to leave their devoted colleague, Mrs. Brant, at the mercy of her antagonistic and cold-blooded husband at such a crisis, and it is to be feared also that Clarence, as a reputed lukewarm partisan, excited no personal sympathy, even from his own party. Howbeit, the deputy agreed to delay Pinckney's journey for a parting interview with his fair hostess.

How far this expressed the real sentiments of Captain Pinckney was never known. Whether his political association with Mrs. Brant had developed into a warmer solicitude, understood or ignored by her,—what were his hopes and aspirations regarding her future,—were by the course of fate never disclosed. A man of easy ethics, but rigid artificialities of honor, flattered and pampered by class prejudice, a so-called "man of the world," with no experience beyond his own limited circle, yet brave and devoted to that, it were well perhaps to leave this last act of his inefficient life as it was accepted by the deputy.

Dismounting he approached the house from the garden. He was already familiar with the low arched doorway which led to the business room, and from which he could gain admittance to the patio, but it so chanced that he entered the dark passage at the moment that Clarence had thrust Susy into the business room, and heard its door shut sharply. For an instant he believed that Mrs. Brant had taken refuge there, but as he cautiously moved forward he heard her voice in the patio beyond. Its accents struck him as pleading; an intense curiosity drew him further along the passage. Suddenly her voice seemed to change to angry denunciation, and the word "Liar" rang upon his ears. It was followed by his own name uttered sardonically by Clarence, the swift rustle of a skirt, the clash of the gate, and then—forgetting everything, he burst into the patio.

Clarence was just turning from the gate with the marks of his wife's hand still red on his white cheek. He saw Captain Pinckney's eyes upon it, and the faint, half-malicious, half-hysteric smile upon his lips. But without a start or gesture of surprise he locked the gate, and turning to him, said with frigid significance,—

"I thank you for returning so promptly, and for recognizing the only thing I now require at your hand."

But Captain Pinckney had recovered his supercilious ease with the significant demand.

"You seem to have had something already from another's hand, sir, but I am at your service," he said lightly.

"You will consider that I have accepted it from you," said Clarence, drawing closer to him with a rigid face. "I suppose it will not be necessary for me to return it—to make you understand me."

"Go on," said Pinckney, flushing slightly. "Make your terms; I am ready."

"But I'm not," said the unexpected voice of the deputy at the grille of the gateway. "Excuse my interfering, gentlemen, but this sort o' thing ain't down in my schedule. I've let this gentleman," pointing to Captain Pinckney, "off for a minit to say 'good-by' to a lady, who I reckon has just ridden off in her buggy with her servant without saying by your leave, but I didn't calkelate to let him inter another business, which, like as not, may prevent me from delivering his body safe and sound into court. You hear me!" As Clarence opened the gate he added, "I don't want ter spoil sport between gents, but it's got to come in after I've done my duty."

"I'll meet you, sir, anywhere, and with what weapons you choose," said Pinckney, turning angrily upon Clarence, "as soon as this farce—for which you and your friends are responsible—is over." He was furious at the intimation that Mrs. Brant had escaped him.

A different thought was in the husband's mind. "But what assurance have I that you are going on with the deputy?" he said with purposely insulting deliberation.

"My word, sir," said Captain Pinckney sharply.

"And if that ain't enuff, there's mine!" said the deputy. "For if this gentleman swerves to the right or left betwixt this and Santa Inez, I'll blow a hole through him myself. And that," he added deprecatingly, "is saying a good deal for a man who doesn't want to spoil sport, and for the matter of that is willing to stand by and see fair play done at Santa Inez any time to-morrow before breakfast."

"Then I can count on you," said Clarence, with a sudden impulse extending his hand.

The man hesitated a moment and then grasped it.

"Well, I wasn't expecting that," he said slowly; "but you look as if you meant business, and if you ain't got anybody else to see you through, I'm thar! I suppose this gentleman will have his friends."

"I shall be there at six with my seconds," said Pinckney curtly. "Lead on."

The gate closed behind them. Clarence stood looking around the empty patio and the silent house, from which it was now plain that the servants had been withdrawn to insure the secrecy of the conspiracy. Cool and collected as he knew he was, he remained for a moment in hesitation. Then the sound of voices came to his ear from the garden room, the light frivolity of Susy's laugh and Hooker's huskier accents. He had forgotten they were there—he had forgotten their existence!

Trusting still to his calmness, he called to Hooker in his usual voice. That gentleman appeared with a face which his attempts to make unconcerned and impassive had, however, only deepened into funereal gravity.

"I have something to attend to," said Clarence, with a faint smile, "and I must ask you and Susy to excuse me for a little while. She knows the house perfectly, and will call the servants from the annex to provide you both with refreshment until I join you a little later." Satisfied from Hooker's manner that they knew nothing of his later interview with Pinckney, he turned away and ascended to his own room.

There he threw himself into an armchair by the dim light of a single candle as if to reflect. But he was conscious, even then, of his own calmness and want of excitement, and that no reflection was necessary. What he had done and what he intended to do was quite clear, there was no alternative suggested or to be even sought after. He had that sense of relief which comes with the climax of all great struggles, even of defeat.

He had never known before how hopeless and continuous had been that struggle until now it was over. He had no fear of tomorrow, he would meet it as he had to-day, with the same singular consciousness of being equal to the occasion. There was even no necessity of preparation for it; his will, leaving his fortune to his wife,—which seemed a slight thing now in this greater separation,—was already in his safe in San Francisco, his pistols were in the next room. He was even slightly disturbed by his own insensibility, and passed into his wife's bedroom partly in the hope of disturbing his serenity by some memento of their past. There was no disorder of flight—everything was in its place, except the drawer of her desk, which was still open, as if she had taken something from it as an afterthought. There were letters and papers there, some of his own and some in Captain Pinckney's handwriting. It did not occur to him to look at them—even to justify himself, or excuse her. He knew that his hatred of Captain Pinckney was not so much that he believed him her lover, as his sudden conviction that she was like him! He was the male of her species—a being antagonistic to himself, whom he could fight, and crush, and revenge himself upon. But most of all he loathed his past, not

Bret Harte

on account of her, but of his own weakness that had made him her dupe and a misunderstood man to his friends. He had been derelict of duty in his unselfish devotion to her; he had stifled his ambition, and underrated his own possibilities. No wonder that others had accepted him at his own valuation. Clarence Brant was a modest man, but the egotism of modesty is more fatal than that of pretension, for it has the haunting consciousness of superior virtue.

He re-entered his own room and again threw himself into his chair. His calm was being succeeded by a physical weariness; he remembered he had not slept the night before, and he ought to take some rest to be fresh in the early morning. Yet he must also show himself before his self-invited guests,—Susy and her husband,—or their suspicions would be aroused. He would try to sleep for a little while in the chair before he went downstairs again. He closed his eyes oddly enough on a dim dreamy recollection of Susy in the old days, in the little madrono hollow where she had once given him a rendezvous. He forgot the maturer and critical uneasiness with which he had then received her coquettish and willful advances, which he now knew was the effect of the growing dominance of Mrs. Peyton over him, and remembered only her bright, youthful eyes, and the kisses he had pressed upon her soft fragrant cheek. The faintness he had felt when waiting in the old rose garden, a few hours ago, seemed to steal on him once more, and to lapse into a pleasant drowsiness. He even seemed again to inhale the perfume of the roses.

"Clarence!"

He started. He had been sleeping, but the voice sounded strangely real.

A light, girlish laugh followed. He sprang to his feet. It was

Susy standing beside him—and Susy even as she looked in the old days!

For with a flash of her old audacity, aided by her familiar knowledge of the house and the bunch of household keys she had found, which dangled from her girdle, as in the old fashion, she had disinterred one of her old frocks from a closet, slipped it on, and unloosening her brown hair had let it fall in rippling waves down her back. It was Susy in her old girlishness, with the instinct of the grown actress in the arrangement of her short skirt over her pretty ankles and the half-conscious pose she had taken.

"Poor dear old Clarence," she said, with dancing eyes; "I might have won a dozen pairs of gloves from you while you slept there. But you're tired, dear old boy, and you've had a hard time of it. No matter; you've shown yourself a man at last, and I'm proud of you."

Half ashamed of the pleasure he felt even in his embarrassment, Clarence stammered, "But this change—this dress."

Susy clapped her hands like a child. "I knew it would surprise you! It's an old frock I wore the year I went away with auntie. I knew where it was hidden, and fished it out again with these keys, Clarence; it seemed so like old times. Lord! when I was with the old servants again, and you didn't come down, I just felt as if I'd never been away, and I just rampaged free. It seemed to me, don't you know, not as if I'd just come, but as if I'd always been right here, and it was you who'd just come. Don't you understand! Just as you came when me and Mary Rogers were here; don't you remember her, Clarence, and how she used to do 'gooseberry' for us? Well, just like that. So I said to Jim, 'I don't know you any more—get!' and I just slipped on this frock and ordered

Manuela around as I used to do—and she in fits of laughter; I reckon, Clarence, she hasn't laughed as much since I left. And then I thought of you—perhaps worried and flustered as yet over things, and the change, and I just slipped into the kitchen and I told old fat Conchita to make some of these tortillas you know,—with sugar and cinnamon sprinkled on top,—and I tied on an apron and brought 'em up to you on a tray with a glass of that old Catalan wine you used to like. Then I sorter felt frightened when I got here, and I didn't hear any noise, and I put the tray down in the hall and peeped in and found you asleep. Sit still, I'll fetch em."

She tripped out into the passage, returning with the tray, which she put on the table beside Clarence, and then standing back a little and with her hands tucked soubrette fashion in the tiny pockets of her apron, gazed at him with a mischievous smile.

It was impossible not to smile back as he nibbled the crisp Mexican cake and drank the old mission wine. And Susy's tongue trilled an accompaniment to his thanks.

"Lord! it seems so nice to be here—just you and me, Clarence—like in the old days—with nobody naggin' and swoopin' round after you. Don't be greedy, Clarence, but give me a cake." She took one and finished the dregs of his glass.

Then sitting on the arm of his chair, she darted a violet ray of half reproach and half mischievousness into his amused and retrospective eyes. "There used to be room for two in that chair, Klarns."

The use of the old childish diminutive for his name seemed to him natural as her familiarity, and he moved a little sideways to make room for her with an instinct of pleasure, but the same sense of irresponsibility that had characterized his reflections. Nevertheless, he looked critically into the mischievous eyes, and said quietly,—

"Where is your husband?"

There was no trace of embarrassment, apology, or even of consciousness in her pretty face as she replied, passing her hand lightly through his hair,—

"Oh, Jim? I've packed him off!"

"Packed him off!" echoed Clarence, slightly astonished.

"Yes, to Fair Plains, full tilt after your wife's buggy. You see, Clarence, after the old cat—that's your wife, please—left, I wanted to make sure she had gone, and wasn't hangin' round to lead you off again with your leg tied to her apron string like a chicken's! No! I said to Jim, 'Just you ride after her until you see she's safe and sound in the down coach from Fair Plains without her knowin' it, and if she's inclined to hang back or wobble any, you post back here and let me know!' I told him I would stay and look after you to see you didn't bolt too!" She laughed, and then added, "But I didn't think I should fall into the old ways so soon, and have such a nice time. Did you, Clarence?"

She looked so irresponsible, sitting there with her face near his, and so childishly, or perhaps thoughtlessly, happy, that he could only admire her levity, and even the slight shock that her flippant allusion to his wife had given him seemed to him only a weakness of his own. After all, was not hers the true philosophy? Why should not these bright eyes see things more clearly than his own? Nevertheless, with his eyes still fixed upon them, he continued,—

"And Jim was willing to go?"

She stopped, with her fingers still lifting a lock of his hair. "Why, yes, you silly—why shouldn't he? I'd like to see him refuse. Why, Lord! Jim will do anything I ask him." She put down the lock of hair, and suddenly looking full into his eyes, said, "That's just the difference between him and me, and you and—that woman!"

"Then you love him!"

"About as much as you love her," she said, with an unaffected laugh; "only he don't wind me around his finger."

No doubt she was right for all her thoughtlessness, and yet he was going to fight about that woman to-morrow! No—he forgot; he was going to fight Captain Pinckney because he was like her!

Susy had put her finger on the crease between his brows which this supposition had made, and tried to rub it out.

"You know it as well as I do, Clarence," she said, with a pretty wrinkling of her own brows, which was her nearest approach to thoughtfulness. "You know you never really liked her, only you thought her ways were grander and more proper than mine, and you know you were always a little bit of a snob and a prig too—dear boy. And Mrs. Peyton was—bless my soul!—a Benham and a planter's daughter, and I—I was only a picked-up orphan! That's where Jim is better than you—now sit still, goosey!—even if I don't like him as much. Oh, I know what you're always thinking, you're thinking we're both exaggerated and theatrical, ain't you? But don't you think it's a heap better to be exaggerated and theatrical about things that are just sentimental and romantic than to be so awfully possessed and overcome about things that are only real? There, you needn't stare at me so! It's true. You've had your fill of grandeur and propriety, and—here you are. And," she added with a little chuckle, as she tucked up her feet and leaned a little closer to him, "here's ME."

He did not speak, but his arm quite unconsciously passed round her small waist.

"You see, Clarence," she went on with equal unconsciousness of the act, "you ought never to have let me go—never! You ought to have kept me here—or run away with me. And you oughtn't to have tried to make me proper. And you oughtn't to have driven me to flirt with that horrid Spaniard, and you oughtn't to have been so horribly cold and severe when I did. And you oughtn't to have made me take up with Jim, who was the only one who thought me his equal. I might have been very silly and capricious; I might have been very vain, but my vanity isn't a bit worse than your pride; my love of praise and applause in the theatre isn't a bit more horrid than your fears of what people might think of you or me. That's gospel truth, isn't it, Clarence? Tell me! Don't look that way and this—look at ME! I ain't poisonous, Clarence. Why, one of your cheeks is redder than the other, Clarence; that's the one that's turned from me. Come," she went on, taking the lapels of his coat between her hands and half shaking him, half drawing him nearer her bright face. "Tell me—isn't it true?"

"I was thinking of you just now when I fell asleep, Susy," he said. He did not know why he said it; he had not intended to tell her, he had only meant to avoid a direct answer to her question; yet even now he went on. "And I thought of you when I was out there in the rose garden waiting to come in here."

"You did?" she said, drawing in her breath. A wave of

delicate pink color came up to her very eyes, it seemed to him as quickly and as innocently as when she was a girl. "And what DID you think, Klarns," she half whispered— "tell me."

He did not speak, but answered her blue eyes and then her lips, as her arms slipped quite naturally around his neck.

*****

The dawn was breaking as Clarence and Jim Hooker emerged together from the gate of the casa. Mr. Hooker looked sleepy. He had found, after his return from Fair Plains, that his host had an early engagement at Santa Inez, and he had insisted upon rising to see him off. It was with difficulty, indeed, that Clarence could prevent his accompanying him. Clarence had not revealed to Susy the night before the real object of his journey, nor did Hooker evidently suspect it, yet when the former had mounted his horse, he hesitated for an instant, extending his hand.

"If I should happen to be detained," he began with a half smile.

But Jim was struggling with a yawn. "That's all right—don't mind us," he said, stretching his arms. Clarence's hesitating hand dropped to his side, and with a light reckless laugh and a half sense of providential relief he galloped away.

What happened immediately thereafter during his solitary ride to Santa Inez, looking back upon it in after years, seemed but a confused recollection, more like a dream. The long stretches of vague distance, gradually opening clearer with the rising sun in an unclouded sky; the meeting with a few early or belated travelers and his unconscious avoidance of them, as if they might know of his object; the black shadows of foreshortened cattle rising before him on the plain and arousing the same uneasy sensation of their being waylaying men; the wondering recognition of houses and landmarks he had long been familiar with; his purposeless attempts to recall the circumstances in which he had known them—all these were like a dream. So, too, were the recollections of the night before, the episode with Susy, already mingled and blended with the memory of their previous past; his futile attempts to look forward to the future, always, however, abandoned with relief at the thought that the next few hours might make them unnecessary. So also was the sudden realization that Santa Inez was before him, when he had thought he was not yet halfway there, and as he dismounted before the Court House his singular feeling—followed, however, by no fear or distress—was that he had come so early to the rendezvous that he was not yet quite prepared for it.

This same sense of unreality pervaded his meeting with the deputy sheriff, at the news that the Federal judge had, as was expected, dismissed the prisoners on their own recognizances, and that Captain Pinckney was at the hotel at breakfast. In the like abstracted manner he replied to the one or two questions of the deputy, exhibited the pistols he had brought with him, and finally accompanied him to a little meadow hidden by trees, below the hotel, where the other principal and his seconds were awaiting them. And here he awoke—clear-eyed, keen, forceful, and intense!

So stimulated were his faculties that his sense of hearing in its acuteness took in every word of the conversation between the seconds, a few paces distant. He heard his adversary's seconds say carelessly to the deputy sheriff, "I presume this is a case where there will be no apology or mediation," and the deputy's reply, "I reckon my man means business, but he seems a little queer." He heard the other second laugh, and say lightly, "They're apt to be so when it's their first time out," followed by the more anxious aside of the other second as the deputy turned away,—"Yes, but by G-d I don't like his looks!" His sense of sight was also so acute that having lost the choice of position, when the coin was tossed, and being turned with his face to the sun, even through the glare he saw, with unerring distinctness of outline, the black-coated figure of his opponent moved into range—saw the perfect outline of his features, and how the easy, supercilious smile, as he threw away his cigar, appeared to drop out of his face with a kind of vacant awe as he faced him. He felt his nerves become as steel as the counting began, and at the word "three," knew he had fired by the recoil of the pistol in his leveled hand, simultaneously with its utterance. And at the same moment, still standing like a rock, he saw his adversary miserably collapse, his legs grotesquely curving inwards under him,—without even the dignity of death in his fall,—and so sink helplessly like a felled bull to the ground. Still erect, and lowering only the muzzle of his pistol, as a thin feather of smoke curled up its shining side, he saw the doctor and seconds run quickly to the heap, try to lift its limp impotence into shape, and let it drop again with the words, "Right through the forehead, by G-d!"

"You've done for him," said the deputy, turning to Clarence with a singular look of curiosity, "and I reckon you had better get out of this mighty quick. They didn't expect it; they're just ragin'; they may round on you—and"—he added, more slowly, "they seem to have just found out who you are."

Even while he was speaking, Clarence, with his quickened ear, heard the words, "One of Hamilton Brant's pups" "Just like his father," from the group around the dead man. He did not hesitate, but walked coolly towards them. Yet a certain fierce pride—which he had never known before—stirred in his veins as their voices hushed and they half recoiled before him.

"Am I to understand from my second, gentlemen," he said, looking round the group, "that you are not satisfied?"

"The fight was square enough," said Pinckney's second in some embarrassment, "but I reckon that he," pointing to the dead man, "did not know who you were."

"Do you mean that he did not know that I was the son of a man proficient in the use of arms?"

"I reckon that's about it," returned the second, glancing at the others.

"I am glad to say, sir, that I have a better opinion of his courage," said Clarence, lifting his hat to the dead body as he turned away.

Yet he was conscious of no remorse, concern, or even pity in his act. Perhaps this was visible in his face, for the group appeared awed by this perfection of the duelist's coolness, and even returned his formal parting salutation with a vague and timid respect. He thanked the deputy, regained the hotel, saddled his horse and galloped away.

But not towards the Rancho. Now that he could think of his future, that had no place in his reflections; even the episode of Susy was forgotten in the new and strange conception of himself and his irresponsibility which had come upon him with the killing of Pinckney and the words of his second. It was his dead father who had stiffened his arm and directed the fatal shot! It was hereditary influences—which others had been so quick to recognize—that had brought about this completing climax of his trouble. How else could he account for it that he—a conscientious, peaceful, sensitive man, tender and forgiving as he had believed himself to be—could now feel so little sorrow or compunction for his culminating act? He had read of successful duelists who were haunted by remorse for their first victim; who retained a terrible consciousness of the appearance of the dead man; he had no such feeling; he had only a grim contentment in the wiped-out inefficient life, and contempt for the limp and helpless body. He suddenly recalled his callousness as a boy when face to face with the victims of the Indian massacre, his sense of fastidious superciliousness in the discovery of the body of Susy's mother!—surely it was the cold blood of his father influencing him ever thus. What had he to do with affection, with domestic happiness, with the ordinary ambitions of man's life—whose blood was frozen at its source! Yet even with this very thought came once more the old inconsistent tenderness he had as a boy lavished upon the almost unknown and fugitive father who had forsaken his childish companionship, and remembered him only by secret gifts. He remembered how he had worshiped him even while the pious padres at San Jose were endeavoring to eliminate this terrible poison from his blood and combat his hereditary instinct in his conflicts with his school-fellows. And it was a part of this inconsistency that, riding away from the scene of his first bloodshed, his eyes were dimmed with moisture, not for his victim, but for the one being who he believed had impelled him to the act.

This and more was in his mind during his long ride to Fair Plains, his journey by coach to the Embarcadero, his midnight passage across the dark waters of the bay, and his re-entrance to San Francisco, but what should be his future was still unsettled.

As he wound round the crest of Russian Hill and looked down again upon the awakened city, he was startled to see that it was fluttering and streaming with bunting. From every public building and hotel, from the roofs of private houses, and even the windows of lonely dwellings, flapped and waved the striped and starry banner. The steady breath of the sea carried it out from masts and yards of ships at their wharves, from the battlements of the forts Alcatraz and Yerba Bueno. He remembered that the ferryman had told him that the news from Fort Sumter had swept the city with a revulsion of patriotic sentiment, and that there was no doubt that the State was saved to the Union. He looked down upon it with haggard, bewildered eyes, and then a strange gasp and fullness of the throat! For afar a solitary bugle had blown the "reveille" at Fort Alcatraz.

Bret Harte

PART II

CHAPTER I

Night at last, and the stir and tumult of a great fight over. Even the excitement that had swept this portion of the battlefield— only a small section of a vaster area of struggle—into which a brigade had marched, held its own, been beaten back, recovered its ground, and pursuing, had passed out of it forever, leaving only its dead behind, and knowing nothing more of that struggle than its own impact and momentum— even this wild excitement had long since evaporated with the stinging smoke of gunpowder, the acrid smell of burning rags from the clothing of a dead soldier fired by a bursting shell, or the heated reek of sweat and leather. A cool breath that seemed to bring back once more the odor of the upturned earthworks along the now dumb line of battle began to move from the suggestive darkness beyond.

But into that awful penetralia of death and silence there was no invasion—there had been no retreat. A few of the wounded had been brought out, under fire, but the others had been left with the dead for the morning light and succor. For it was known that in that horrible obscurity, riderless horses, frantic with the smell of blood, galloped wildly here and there, or, maddened by wounds, plunged furiously at the intruder; that the wounded soldier, still armed, could not always distinguish friend from foe or from the ghouls of camp followers who stripped the dead in the darkness and struggled with the dying. A shot or two heard somewhere in that obscurity counted as nothing with the long fusillade that had swept it in the daytime; the passing of a single life, more or less, amounted to little in the long roll-call of the day's slaughter.

But with the first beams of the morning sun—and the slowly moving "relief detail" from the camp—came a weird half-resurrection of that ghastly field. Then it was that the long rays of sunlight, streaming away a mile beyond the battle line, pointed out the first harvest of the dead where the reserves had been posted. There they lay in heaps and piles, killed by solid shot or bursting shells that had leaped the battle line to plunge into the waiting ranks beyond. As the sun lifted higher its beams fell within the range of musketry fire, where the dead lay thicker,—even as they had fallen when killed outright,—with arms extended and feet at all angles to the field. As it touched these dead upturned faces, strangely enough it brought out no expression of pain or anguish—but rather as if death had arrested them only in surprise and awe. It revealed on the lips of those who had been mortally wounded and had turned upon their side the relief which death had brought their suffering, sometimes shown in a faint smile. Mounting higher, it glanced upon the actual battle line, curiously curving for the shelter of walls, fences, and breastworks, and here the dead lay, even as when they lay and fired, their faces prone in the grass but their muskets still resting across the breastworks. Exposed to grape and canister from the battery on the ridge, death had come to them mercifully also—through the head and throat. And now the whole field lay bare in the sunlight, broken with grotesque shadows cast from sitting, crouching, half-recumbent but always rigid figures, which might have been effigies on their own monuments. One half-kneeling soldier, with head bowed between his stiffened hands, might have stood for a carven figure of Grief at the feet of his dead comrade. A captain, shot through the brain in the act of mounting a wall, lay sideways half across it, his lips parted with a word of command; his sword still pointing over the barrier the way that they should go.

But it was not until the sun had mounted higher that it struck the central horror of the field and seemed to linger there in dazzling persistence, now and then returning to it in startling flashes that it might be seen of men and those who brought succor. A tiny brook had run obliquely near the battle line. It was here that, the night before the battle, friend and foe had filled their canteens side by side with soldierly reckless-ness—or perhaps a higher instinct—purposely ignoring each other's presence; it was here that the wounded had afterwards crept, crawled, and dragged themselves, here they had pushed, wrangled, striven, and fought for a draught of that precious fluid which assuaged the thirst of their wounds—or happily put them out of their misery forever; here overborne, crushed, suffocated by numbers, pouring their own blood into the flood, and tumbling after it with their helpless bodies, they dammed the stream, until recoiling, red and angry, it had burst its banks and overflowed the cotton-field in a broad pool that now sparkled in the sunlight. But below this human dam—a mile away—where the brook still crept sluggishly, the ambulance horses sniffed and started from it.

The detail moved on slowly, doing their work expeditiously, and apparently callously, but really only with that mechanical movement that saves emotion. Only once they were moved to an outbreak of indignation,—the discovery of the body of an officer whose pockets were turned inside out, but whose hand was still tightly grasped on his buttoned waistcoat, as if resisting the outrage that had been done while still in life. As the men disengaged the stiffened hand something slipped from the waistcoat to the ground. The corporal picked it up and handed it to his officer. It was a sealed packet. The officer received it with the carelessness which long experience of these pathetic missives from the dying to their living relations had induced, and dropped it in the pocket of his tunic, with the half-dozen others that he had picked up that morning, and moved on with the detail. A little further on they halted, in the attitude of attention, as a mounted officer appeared, riding slowly down the line.

There was something more than the habitual respect of their superior in their faces as he came forward. For it was the general who had commanded the brigade the day before,— the man who had leaped with one bound into the foremost rank of military leaders. It was his invincible spirit that had led the advance, held back defeat against overwhelming numbers, sustained the rally, impressed his subordinate officers with his own undeviating purpose, and even infused them with an almost superstitious belief in his destiny of success. It was this man who had done what it was deemed impossible to do,—what even at the time it was thought unwise and unstrategic to do,—who had held a weak position, of apparently no importance, under the mandate of an incomprehensible order from his superior, which at best asked only for a sacrifice and was rewarded with a victory. He had decimated his brigade, but the wounded and dying had cheered him as he passed, and the survivors had pursued the enemy until the bugle called them back. For such a record he looked still too young and scholarly, albeit his handsome face was dark and energetic, and his manner taciturn.

His quick eye had already caught sight of the rifled body of the officer, and contracted. As the captain of the detail saluted him he said curtly,—

"I thought the orders were to fire upon any one desecrating the dead?"

"They are, General; but the hyenas don't give us a chance. That's all yonder poor fellow saved from their claws," replied the officer, as he held up the sealed packet. "It has no address."

The general took it, examined the envelope, thrust it into his belt, and said,—

"I will take charge of it."

The sound of horses' hoofs came from the rocky roadside beyond the brook. Both men turned. A number of field officers were approaching.

"The division staff," said the captain, in a lower voice, falling back.

They came slowly forward, a central figure on a gray horse leading here—as in history. A short, thick-set man with a grizzled beard closely cropped around an inscrutable mouth, and the serious formality of a respectable country deacon in his aspect, which even the major-generals blazon on the shoulder-strap of his loose tunic on his soldierly seat in the saddle could not entirely obliterate. He had evidently perceived the general of brigade, and quickened his horse as the latter drew up. The staff followed more leisurely, but still with some curiosity, to witness the meeting of the first general of the army with the youngest. The division general saluted, but almost instantly withdrew his leathern gauntlet, and offered his bared hand to the brigadier. The words of heroes are scant. The drawn-up detail, the waiting staff listened. This was all they heard:—

"Halleck tells me you're from California?"

"Yes, General."

"Ah! I lived there, too, in the early days."

"Wonderful country. Developed greatly since my time, I suppose?"

"Yes, General."

"Great resources; finest wheat-growing country in the world, sir. You don't happen to know what the actual crop was this year?"

"Hardly, General! but something enormous."

"Yes, I have always said it would be. Have a cigar?"

He handed his cigar-case to the brigadier. Then he took one himself, lighted it at the smouldering end of the one he had taken from his mouth, was about to throw the stump carelessly down, but, suddenly recollecting himself, leaned over his horse, and dropped it carefully a few inches away from the face of a dead soldier. Then, straightening himself in the saddle, he shoved his horse against the brigadier, moving him a little further on, while a slight movement of his hand kept the staff from following.

"A heavy loss here!"

"I'm afraid so, General."

"It couldn't be helped. We had to rush in your brigade to gain time, and occupy the enemy, until we could change front."

The young general looked at the shrewd, cold eyes of his chief.

"Change front?" he echoed.

"Yes. Before a gun was fired, we discovered that the enemy was in complete possession of all our plans, and knew every detail of our forward movement. All had to be changed."

The younger man now instantly understood the incomprehensible order of the day before.

The general of division continued, with his first touch of official formality,—

"You understand, therefore, General Brant, that in the face of this extraordinary treachery, the utmost vigilance is required, and a complete surveillance of your camp followers and civilians, to detect the actual spy within our lines, or the traitor we are harboring, who has become possessed of this information. You will overhaul your brigade, and weed out all suspects, and in the position which you are to take to-morrow, and the plantation you will occupy, you will see that your private quarters, as well as your lines, are cleared of all but those you can vouch for."

He reined in his horse, again extended his hand, saluted, and rejoined his staff.

Brigadier-General Clarence Brant remained for a moment with his head bent in thoughtful contemplation of the coolness of his veteran chief under this exciting disclosure, and the strategy with which he had frustrated the traitor's success. Then his eye caught the sealed packet in his belt. He mechanically drew it out, and broke the seal. The envelope was filled with papers and memorandums. But as he looked at them his face darkened and his brow knit. He glanced quickly around him. The staff had trotted away; the captain and his detail were continuing their work at a little distance. He took a long breath, for he was holding in his hand a tracing of their camp, even of the position he was to occupy tomorrow, and a detailed account of the movements, plans, and force of the whole division as had been arranged in council of war the day before the battle! But there was no indication of the writer or his intentions.

He thrust the papers hurriedly back into the envelope, but placed it, this time, in his breast. He galloped towards the captain.

"Let me see again the officer from whom you took that packet!"

The captain led him to where the body lay, with others, extended more decently on the grass awaiting removal. General Brant with difficulty repressed an ejaculation.

"Why, it's one of our own men," he said quickly.

"Yes, General. They say it's Lieutenant Wainwright, a regular, of the paymaster general's department."

"Then what was he doing here?" asked General Brant sternly.

"I can't make out, sir, unless he went into the last advance as a volunteer. Wanted to see the fight, I suppose. He was a dashing fellow, a West Pointer,—and a Southerner, too,—a Virginian."

"A Southerner!" echoed Brant quickly.

"Yes, sir."

"Search him again," said Brant quietly. He had recovered his usual coolness, and as the captain again examined the body, he took out his tablets and wrote a few lines. It was an order to search the quarters of Lieutenant Wainwright and bring all papers, letters, and documents to him. He then beckoned one of the detail towards him. "Take that to the provost marshal at once. Well, Captain," he added calmly, as the officer again approached him, "what do you find?"

"Only this, sir," returned the captain, with a half smile, producing a small photograph. "I suppose it was overlooked, too."

He handed it to Brant.

There was a sudden fixing of his commanding officer's eyes, but his face did not otherwise change.

"It's the usual find, General. Always a photograph! But this time a handsome woman!"

"Very," said Clarence Brant quietly. It was the portrait of his own wife.

CHAPTER II

Nevertheless, so complete was his control of voice and manner that, as he rode on to his quarters, no one would have dreamed that General Brant had just looked upon the likeness of the wife from whom he had parted in anger four years ago. Still less would they have suspected the strange fear that came upon him that in some way she was connected with the treachery he had just discovered. He had heard from her only once, and then through her late husband's lawyer, in regard to her Californian property, and believed that she had gone to her relations in Alabama, where she had identified herself with the Southern cause, even to the sacrifice of her private fortune. He had heard her name mentioned in the Southern press as a fascinating society leader, and even coadjutrix of Southern politicians,—but he had no reason to believe that she had taken so active or so desperate a part in the struggle. He tried to think that his uneasiness sprang from his recollection of the previous treachery of Captain Pinckney, and the part that she had played in the Californian conspiracy, although he had long since acquitted her of the betrayal of any nearer trust. But there was a fateful similarity in the two cases. There was no doubt that this Lieutenant Wainwright was a traitor in the camp,—that he had succumbed to the usual sophistry of his class in regard to his superior allegiance to his native State. But was there the inducement of another emotion, or was the photograph only

Bret Harte

the souvenir of a fascinating priestess of rebellion, whom the dead man had met? There was perhaps less of feeling than scorn in the first suggestion, but he was nevertheless relieved when the provost marshal found no other incriminating papers in Wainwright's effects. Nor did he reveal to the division general the finding of the photograph. It was sufficient to disclose the work of the traitor without adding what might be a clue to his wife's participation in it, near or remote. There was risk enough in the former course,—which his duty made imperative. He hardly dared to think of the past day's slaughter, which—there was no doubt now—had been due to the previous work of the spy, and how his brigade had been selected—by the irony of Fate—to suffer for and yet retrieve it. If she had had a hand in this wicked plot, ought he to spare her? Or was his destiny and hers to be thus monstrously linked together?

Luckily, however, the expiation of the chief offender and the timely discovery of his papers enabled the division commander to keep the affair discreetly silent, and to enjoin equal secrecy on the part of Brant. The latter, however, did not relax his vigilance, and after the advance the next day he made a minute inspection of the ground he was to occupy, its approaches and connections with the outlying country, and the rebel lines; increased the stringency of picket and sentry regulations, and exercised a rigid surveillance of non-combatants and civilians within the lines, even to the lowest canteener or camp follower. Then he turned his attention to the house he was to occupy as his headquarters.

It was a fine specimen of the old colonial planter's house, with its broad veranda, its great detached offices and negro quarters, and had, thus far, escaped the ravages and billeting of the war. It had been occupied by its owner up to a few days before the engagement, and so great had been the confidence of the enemy in their success that it had been used as the Confederate headquarters on the morning of the decisive battle. Jasmine and rose, unstained by the sulphur of gunpowder, twined around its ruined columns and half hid the recessed windows; the careless flower garden was still in its unkempt and unplucked luxuriance; the courtyard before the stables alone showed marks of the late military occupancy, and was pulverized by the uneasy horse-hoofs of the waiting staff. But the mingled impress of barbaric prodigality with patriarchal simplicity was still there in the domestic arrangements of a race who lived on half equal familiarity with strangers and their own servants.

The negro servants still remained, with a certain cat-like fidelity to the place, and adapted themselves to the Northern invaders with a childlike enjoyment of the novelty of change. Brant, nevertheless, looked them over with an experienced eye, and satisfied himself of their trustworthiness; there was the usual number of "boys," gray-haired and grizzled in body service, and the "mammys" and "aunties" of the kitchen. There were two or three rooms in the wing which still contained private articles, pictures and souvenirs of the family, and a "young lady's" boudoir, which Brant, with characteristic delicacy, kept carefully isolated and intact from his military household, and accessible only to the family servants. The room he had selected for himself was nearest it,—a small, plainly furnished apartment, with an almost conventual simplicity in its cold, white walls and draperies, and the narrow, nun-like bed. It struck him that it might have belonged to some prim elder daughter or maiden aunt, who had acted as housekeeper, as it commanded the wing and servants' offices, with easy access to the central hall.

There followed a week of inactivity in which Brant felt a singular resemblance in this Southern mansion to the old casa at Robles. The afternoon shadows of the deep verandas recalled the old monastic gloom of the Spanish house, which

Bret Harte

even the presence of a lounging officer or waiting orderly could not entirely dissipate, and the scent of the rose and jasmine from his windows overcame him with sad memories. He began to chafe under this inaction, and long again for the excitement of the march and bivouac, in which, for the past four years, he had buried his past.

He was sitting one afternoon alone before his reports and dispatches, when this influence seemed so strong that he half impulsively laid them aside to indulge in along reverie. He was recalling his last day at Robles, the early morning duel with Pinckney, the return to San Francisco, and the sudden resolution which sent him that day across the continent to offer his services to the Government. He remembered his delay in the Western town, where a volunteer regiment was being recruited, his entrance into it as a private, his rapid selection, through the force of his sheer devotion and intelligent concentration, to the captaincy of his company; his swift promotion on hard-fought fields to the head of the regiment, and the singular success that had followed his resistless energy, which left him no time to think of anything but his duty. The sudden intrusion of his wife upon his career now, even in this accidental and perhaps innocent way, had seriously unsettled him.

The shadows were growing heavier and deeper, it lacked only a few moments of the sunset bugle, when he was recalled to himself by that singular instinctive consciousness, common to humanity, of being intently looked at. He turned quickly,—the door behind him closed softly. He rose and slipped into the hall. The tall figure of a woman was going down the passage. She was erect and graceful; but, as she turned towards the door leading to the offices, he distinctly saw the gaudily turbaned head and black silhouette of a negress. Nevertheless, he halted a moment at the door of the next room.

"See who that woman is who has just passed, Mr. Martin. She doesn't seem to belong to the house."

The young officer rose, put on his cap, and departed. In a few moments he returned.

"Was she tall, sir, of a good figure, and very straight?"

"Yes."

"She is a servant of our neighbors, the Manlys, who occasionally visits the servants here. A mulatto, I think."

Brant reflected. Many of the mulattoes and negresses were of good figure, and the habit of carrying burdens on their heads gave them a singularly erect carriage.

The lieutenant looked at his chief.

"Have you any orders to give concerning her, General?"

"No," said Brant, after a moment's pause, and turned away.

The officer smiled. It seemed a good story to tell at mess of this human weakness of his handsome, reserved, and ascetic-looking leader.

A few mornings afterwards Brant was interrupted over his reports by the almost abrupt entrance of the officer of the day. His face was flushed, and it was evident that only the presence of his superior restrained his excitement. He held a paper in his hand.

"A lady presents this order and pass from Washington, countersigned by the division general."

"A lady?"

"Yes, sir, she is dressed as such. But she has not only declined the most ordinary civilities and courtesies we have offered her, but she has insulted Mr. Martin and myself grossly, and demands to be shown to you—alone."

Brant took the paper. It was a special order from the President, passing Miss Matilda Faulkner through the Federal lines to visit her uncle's home, known as "Gray Oaks," now held and occupied as the headquarters of Brant's Brigade, in order to arrange for the preservation and disposal of certain family effects and private property that still remained there, or to take and carry away such property; and invoking all necessary aid and assistance from the United States forces in such occupancy. It was countersigned by the division commander. It was perfectly regular and of undoubted authenticity. He had heard of passes of this kind,—the terror of the army,—issued in Washington under some strange controlling influence and against military protest; but he did not let his subordinate see the uneasiness with which it filled him.

"Show her in," he said quietly.

But she had already entered, brushing scornfully past the officer, and drawing her skirt aside, as if contaminated: a very pretty Southern girl, scornful and red-lipped, clad in a gray riding-habit, and still carrying her riding-whip clenched ominously in her slim, gauntleted hand!

"You have my permit in your hand," she said brusquely, hardly raising her eyes to Brant. "I suppose it's all straight enough,—and even if it isn't, I don't reckon to be kept waiting with those hirelings."

"Your 'permit' is 'straight' enough, Miss Faulkner," said Brant, slowly reading her name from the document before him. "But, as it does not seem to include permission to insult my officers, you will perhaps allow them first to retire."

He made a sign to the officer, who passed out of the door.

As it closed, he went on, in a gentle but coldly unimpassioned voice,—

"I perceive you are a Southern lady, and therefore I need not remind you that it is not considered good form to treat even the slaves of those one does not like uncivilly, and I must, therefore, ask you to keep your active animosity for myself."

The young girl lifted her eyes. She had evidently not expected to meet a man so young, so handsome, so refined, and so coldly invincible in manner. Still less was she prepared for that kind of antagonism. In keeping up her preconcerted attitude towards the "Northern hireling," she had been met with official brusqueness, contemptuous silence, or aggrieved indignation,—but nothing so exasperating as this. She even fancied that this elegant but sardonic-looking soldier was mocking her. She bit her red lip, but, with a scornful gesture of her riding-whip, said,—

"I reckon that your knowledge of Southern ladies is, for certain reasons, not very extensive."

"Pardon me; I have had the honor of marrying one."

Apparently more exasperated than before, she turned upon him abruptly.

"You say my pass is all right. Then I presume I may attend to the business that brought me here."

"Certainly; but you will forgive me if I imagined that an expression of contempt for your hosts was a part of it."

He rang a bell on the table. It was responded to by an orderly.

"Send all the household servants here."

The room was presently filled with the dusky faces of the negro retainers. Here and there was the gleaming of white teeth, but a majority of the assembly wore the true negro serious acceptance of the importance of "an occasion." One or two even affected an official and soldierly bearing. And, as he fully expected, there were several glances of significant recognition of the stranger.

"You will give," said Brant sternly, "every aid and attention to the wants of this young lady, who is here to represent the interests of your old master. As she will be entirely dependent upon you in all things connected with her visit here, see to it that she does not have to complain to me of any inattention,—or be obliged to ask for other assistance."

As Miss Faulkner, albeit a trifle paler in the cheek, but as scornful as ever, was about to follow the servants from the room, Brant stopped her, with a coldly courteous gesture.

"You will understand, therefore, Miss Faulkner, that you have your wish, and that you will not be exposed to any contact with the members of my military family, nor they with you."

"Am I then to be a prisoner in this house—and under a free pass of your—President?" she said indignantly.

"By no means! You are free to come and go, and see whom

you please. I have no power to control your actions. But I have the power to control theirs."

She swept furiously from the room.

"That is quite enough to fill her with a desire to flirt with every man here," said Brant to himself, with a faint smile; "but I fancy they have had a taste enough of her quality."

Nevertheless he sat down and wrote a few lines to the division commander, pointing out that he had already placed the owner's private property under strict surveillance, that it was cared for and perfectly preserved by the household servants, and that the pass was evidently obtained as a subterfuge.

To this he received a formal reply, regretting that the authorities at Washington still found it necessary to put this kind of risk and burden on the army in the field, but that the order emanated from the highest authority, and must be strictly obeyed. At the bottom of the page was a characteristic line in pencil in the general's own hand—"Not the kind that is dangerous."

A flush mounted Brant's cheeks, as if it contained not only a hidden, but a personal significance. He had thought of his own wife!

Singularly enough, a day or two later, at dinner, the conversation turned upon the intense sectional feeling of Southern women, probably induced by their late experiences. Brant, at the head of the table, in his habitual abstraction, was scarcely following the somewhat excited diction of Colonel Strangeways, one of his staff.

"No, sir," reiterated that indignant warrior, "take my word

for it! A Southern woman isn't to be trusted on this point, whether as a sister, sweetheart, or wife. And when she is trusted, she's bound to get the better of the man in any of those relations!"

The dead silence that followed, the ominous joggle of a glass at the speaker's elbow, the quick, sympathetic glance that Brant instinctively felt was directed at his own face, and the abrupt change of subject, could not but arrest his attention, even if he had overlooked the speech. His face, however, betrayed nothing. It had never, however, occurred to him before that his family affairs might be known—neither had he ever thought of keeping them a secret. It seemed so purely a personal and private misfortune, that he had never dreamed of its having any public interest. And even now he was a little ashamed of what he believed was his sensitiveness to mere conventional criticism, which, with the instinct of a proud man, he had despised.

He was not far wrong in his sardonic intuition of the effect of his prohibition upon Miss Faulkner's feelings. Certainly that young lady, when not engaged in her mysterious occupation of arranging her uncle's effects, occasionally was seen in the garden, and in the woods beyond. Although her presence was the signal for the "oblique" of any lounging "shoulder strap," or the vacant "front" of a posted sentry, she seemed to regard their occasional proximity with less active disfavor. Once, when she had mounted the wall to gather a magnolia blossom, the chair by which she had ascended rolled over, leaving her on the wall. At a signal from the guard-room, two sappers and miners appeared carrying a scaling-ladder, which they placed silently against the wall, and as silently withdrew. On another occasion, the same spirited young lady, whom Brant was satisfied would have probably imperiled her life under fire in devotion to her cause, was brought ignominiously to bay in the field by that most appalling of domestic animals, the wandering and untrammeled cow! Brant could not help smiling as he heard the quick, harsh call to "Turn out, guard," saw the men march stolidly with fixed bayonets to the vicinity of the affrighted animal, who fled, leaving the fair stranger to walk shamefacedly to the house. He was surprised, however, that she should have halted before his door, and with tremulous indignation, said,—

"I thank you, sir, for your chivalrousness in turning a defenseless woman into ridicule."

"I regret, Miss Faulkner," began Brant gravely, "that you should believe that I am able to control the advances of farmyard cattle as easily as"—But he stopped, as he saw that the angry flash of her blue eyes, as she darted past him, was set in tears. A little remorseful on the following day, he added a word to his ordinary cap-lifting when she went by, but she retained a reproachful silence. Later in the day, he received from her servant a respectful request for an interview, and was relieved to find that she entered his presence with no trace of her former aggression, but rather with the resignation of a deeply injured, yet not entirely unforgiving, woman.

"I thought," she began coldly, "that I ought to inform you that I would probably be able to conclude my business here by the day after to-morrow, and that you would then be relieved of my presence. I am aware—indeed," she added, bitterly, "I could scarcely help perceiving, that it has been an exceedingly irksome one."

"I trust," began Brant coldly, "that no gentleman of my command has"—

"No!"

She interrupted him quickly, with a return of her former manner, and a passionate sweep of the hand.

"Do you suppose for a moment that I am speaking—that I am even thinking—of them? What are they to me?"

"Thank you. I am glad to know that they are nothing; and that I may now trust that you have consulted my wishes, and have reserved your animosity solely for me," returned Brant quietly. "That being so, I see no reason for your hurrying your departure in the least."

She rose instantly.

"I have," she said slowly, controlling herself with a slight effort, "found some one who will take my duty off my hands. She is a servant of one of your neighbors,—who is an old friend of my uncle's. The woman is familiar with the house, and our private property. I will give her full instructions to act for me, and even an authorization in writing, if you prefer it. She is already in the habit of coming here; but her visits will give you very little trouble. And, as she is a slave, or, as you call it, I believe, a chattel, she will be already quite accustomed to the treatment which her class are in the habit of receiving from Northern hands."

Without waiting to perceive the effect of her Parthian shot, she swept proudly out of the room.

"I wonder what she means," mused Brant, as her quick step died away in the passage. "One thing is certain,—a woman like that is altogether too impulsive for a spy."

Later, in the twilight, he saw her walking in the garden. There was a figure at her side. A little curious, he examined it more closely from his window. It was already familiar to him,—the erect, shapely form of his neighbor's servant. A thoughtful look passed over his face as he muttered,—"So this is to be her deputy."

Bret Harte

CHAPTER III

Called to a general council of officers at divisional headquarters the next day, Brant had little time for further
speculation regarding his strange guest, but a remark from
the division commander, that he preferred to commit the
general plan of a movement then under discussion to their
memories rather than to written orders in the ordinary
routine, seemed to show that his chief still suspected the
existence of a spy. He, therefore, told him of his late
interview with Miss Faulkner, and her probable withdrawal
in favor of a mulatto neighbor. The division commander
received the information with indifference.

"They're much too clever to employ a hussy like that, who
shows her hand at every turn, either as a spy or a messenger
of spies,—and the mulattoes are too stupid, to say nothing of
their probable fidelity to us. No, General, if we are watched,
it is by an eagle, and not a mocking-bird. Miss Faulkner has
nothing worse about her than her tongue; and there isn't the
nigger blood in the whole South that would risk a noose for
her, or for any of their masters or mistresses!"

It was, therefore, perhaps, with some mitigation of his usual
critical severity that he saw her walking before him alone in the
lane as he rode home to quarters. She was apparently lost in a
half-impatient, half-moody reverie, which even the trotting

hoof-beats of his own and his orderly's horse had not disturbed. From time to time she struck the myrtle hedge beside her with the head of a large flower which hung by its stalk from her listless hands, or held it to her face as if to inhale its perfume. Dismissing his orderly by a side path, he rode gently forward, but, to his surprise, without turning, or seeming to be aware of his presence, she quickened her pace, and even appeared to look from side to side for some avenue of escape. If only to mend matters, he was obliged to ride quickly forward to her side, where he threw himself from his horse, flung the reins on his arm, and began to walk beside her. She at first turned a slightly flushed cheek away from him, and then looked up with a purely simulated start of surprise.

"I am afraid," he said gently, "that I am the first to break my own orders in regard to any intrusion on your privacy. But I wanted to ask you if I could give you any aid whatever in the change you think of making."

He was quite sincere,—had been touched by her manifest disturbance, and, despite his masculine relentlessness of criticism, he had an intuition of feminine suffering that was in itself feminine.

"Meaning, that you are in a hurry to get rid of me," she said curtly, without raising her eyes.

"Meaning that I only wish to expedite a business which I think is unpleasant to you, but which I believe you have undertaken from unselfish devotion."

The scant expression of a reserved nature is sometimes more attractive to women than the most fluent vivacity. Possibly there was also a melancholy grace in this sardonic soldier's manner that affected her, for she looked up, and said impulsively,—

"You think so?"

But he met her eager eyes with some surprise.

"I certainly do," he replied more coldly. "I can imagine your feelings on finding your uncle's home in the possession of your enemies, and your presence under the family roof only a sufferance. I can hardly believe it a pleasure to you, or a task you would have accepted for yourself alone."

"But," she said, turning towards him wickedly, "what if I did it only to excite my revenge; what if I knew it would give me courage to incite my people to carry war into your own homes; to make you of the North feel as I feel, and taste our bitterness?"

"I could easily understand that, too," he returned, with listless coldness, "although I don't admit that revenge is an unmixed pleasure, even to a woman."

"A woman!" she repeated indignantly. "There is no sex in a war like this."

"You are spoiling your flower," he said quietly. "It is very pretty, and a native one, too; not an invader, or even transplanted. May I look at it?"

She hesitated, half recoiling for an instant, and her hand trembled. Then, suddenly and abruptly she said, with a hysteric little laugh, "Take it, then," and almost thrust it in his hand.

It certainly was a pretty flower, not unlike a lily in appearance, with a bell-like cup and long anthers covered with a fine pollen, like red dust. As he lifted it to his face, to inhale its perfume, she uttered a slight cry, and snatched it from his hand.

"There!" she said, with the same nervous laugh. "I knew you would; I ought to have warned you. The pollen comes off so easily, and leaves a stain. And you've got some on your cheek. Look!" she continued, taking her handkerchief from her pocket and wiping his cheek; "see there!" The delicate cambric showed a blood-red streak.

"It grows in a swamp," she continued, in the same excited strain; "we call it dragon's teeth,—like the kind that was sown in the story, you know. We children used to find it, and then paint our faces and lips with it. We called it our rouge. I was almost tempted to try it again when I found it just now. It took me back so to the old times."

Following her odd manner rather than her words, as she turned her face towards him suddenly, Brant was inclined to think that she had tried it already, so scarlet was her cheek. But it presently paled again under his cold scrutiny.

"You must miss the old times," he said calmly. "I am afraid you found very little of them left, except in these flowers."

"And hardly these," she said bitterly. "Your troops had found a way through the marsh, and had trampled down the bushes."

Brant's brow clouded. He remembered that the brook, which had run red during the fight, had lost itself in this marsh. It did not increase his liking for this beautiful but blindly vicious animal at his side, and even his momentary pity for her was fading fast. She was incorrigible. They walked on for a few moments in silence.

"You said," she began at last, in a gentler and even hesitating voice, "that your wife was a Southern woman."

He checked an irritated start with difficulty.

"I believe I did," he said coldly, as if he regretted it.

"And of course you taught her YOUR gospel,—the gospel according to St. Lincoln. Oh, I know," she went on hurriedly, as if conscious of his irritation and seeking to allay it. "She was a woman and loved you, and thought with your thoughts and saw only with your eyes. Yes, that's the way with us,—I suppose we all do it!" she added bitterly.

"She had her own opinions," said Brant briefly, as he recovered himself.

Nevertheless, his manner so decidedly closed all further discussion that there was nothing left for the young girl but silence. But it was broken by her in a few moments in her old contemptuous voice and manner.

"Pray don't trouble yourself to accompany me any further, General Brant. Unless, of course, you are afraid I may come across some of your—your soldiers. I promise you I won't eat them."

"I am afraid you must suffer my company a little longer, Miss Faulkner, on account of those same soldiers," returned Brant gravely. "You may not know that this road, in which I find you, takes you through a cordon of pickets. If you were alone you would be stopped, questioned, and, failing to give the password, you would be detained, sent to the guard-house, and"—he stopped, and fixed his eyes on her keenly as he added, "and searched."

"You would not dare to search a woman!" she said

indignantly, although her flush gave way to a slight pallor.

"You said just now that there should be no sex in a war like this," returned Brant carelessly, but without abating his scrutinizing gaze.

"Then it IS war?" she said quickly, with a white, significant face.

His look of scrutiny turned to one of puzzled wonder. But at the same moment there was the flash of a bayonet in the hedge, a voice called "Halt!" and a soldier stepped into the road.

General Brant advanced, met the salute of the picket with a few formal words, and then turned towards his fair companion, as another soldier and a sergeant joined the group.

"Miss Faulkner is new to the camp, took the wrong turning, and was unwittingly leaving the lines when I joined her." He fixed his eyes intently on her now colorless face, but she did not return his look. "You will show her the shortest way to quarters," he continued, to the sergeant, "and should she at any time again lose her way, you will again conduct her home,—but without detaining or reporting her."

He lifted his cap, remounted his horse, and rode away, as the young girl, with a proud, indifferent step, moved down the road with the sergeant. A mounted officer passed him and saluted,—it was one of his own staff. From some strange instinct, he knew that he had witnessed the scene, and from some equally strange intuition he was annoyed by it. But he continued his way, visiting one or two outposts, and returned by a long detour to his quarters. As he stepped upon the veranda he saw Miss Faulkner at the bottom of the garden talking with some one across the hedge. By the aid of his

Bret Harte

glass he could recognize the shapely figure of the mulatto woman which he had seen before. But by its aid he also discovered that she was carrying a flower exactly like the one which Miss Faulkner still held in her hand. Had she been with Miss Faulkner in the lane, and if so, why had she disappeared when he came up? Impelled by something stronger than mere curiosity, he walked quickly down the garden, but she evidently had noticed him, for she as quickly disappeared. Not caring to meet Miss Faulkner again, he retraced his steps, resolving that he would, on the first opportunity, personally examine and interrogate this new visitor. For if she were to take Miss Faulkner's place in a subordinate capacity, this precaution was clearly within his rights.

He re-entered his room and seated himself at his desk before the dispatches, orders, and reports awaiting him. He found himself, however, working half mechanically, and recurring to his late interview with Miss Faulkner in the lane. If she had any inclination to act the spy, or to use her position here as a means of communicating with the enemy's lines, he thought he had thoroughly frightened her. Nevertheless, now, for the first time, he was inclined to accept his chief's opinion of her. She was not only too clumsy and inexperienced, but she totally lacked the self-restraint of a spy. Her nervous agitation in the lane was due to something more disturbing than his mere possible intrusion upon her confidences with the mulatto. The significance of her question, "Then it IS war?" was at best a threat, and that implied hesitation. He recalled her strange allusion to his wife; was it merely the outcome of his own foolish confession on their first interview, or was it a concealed ironical taunt? Being satisfied, however, that she was not likely to imperil his public duty in any way, he was angry with himself for speculating further. But, although he still felt towards her the same antagonism she had at first provoked, he was conscious that she was beginning to exercise a strange fascination over him.

Dismissing her at last with an effort, he finished his work and then rose, and unlocking a closet, took out a small dispatch-box, to which he intended to intrust a few more important orders and memoranda. As he opened it with a key on his watch-chain, he was struck with a faint perfume that seemed to come from it,—a perfume that he remembered. Was it the smell of the flower that Miss Faulkner carried, or the scent of the handkerchief with which she had wiped his cheek, or a mingling of both? Or was he under some spell to think of that wretched girl, and her witch-like flower? He leaned over the box and suddenly started. Upon the outer covering of a dispatch was a singular blood-red streak! He examined it closely,—it was the powdery stain of the lily pollen,—exactly as he had seen it on her handkerchief.

There could be no mistake. He passed his finger over the stain; he could still feel the slippery, infinitesimal powder of the pollen. It was not there when he had closed the box that morning; it was impossible that it should be there unless the box had been opened in his absence. He re-examined the contents of the box; the papers were all there. More than that, they were papers of no importance except to him personally; contained no plans nor key to any military secret; he had been far too wise to intrust any to the accidents of this alien house. The prying intruder, whoever it was, had gained nothing! But there was unmistakably the attempt! And the existence of a would-be spy within the purlieus of the house was equally clear.

He called an officer from the next room.

"Has any one been here since my absence?"

"No, General."

"Has any one passed through the hall?"

He had fully anticipated the answer, as the subaltern replied, "Only the women servants."

He re-entered the room. Closing the door, he again carefully examined the box, his table, the papers upon it, the chair before it, and even the Chinese matting on the floor, for any further indication of the pollen. It hardly seemed possible that any one could have entered the room with the flower in their hand without scattering some of the tell-tale dust elsewhere; it was too large a flower to be worn on the breast or in the hair. Again, no one would have dared to linger there long enough to have made an examination of the box, with an officer in the next room, and the sergeant passing. The box had been removed, and the examination made elsewhere!

An idea seized him. Miss Faulkner was still absent, the mulatto had apparently gone home. He quickly mounted the staircase, but instead of entering his room, turned suddenly aside into the wing which had been reserved. The first door yielded as he turned its knob gently and entered a room which he at once recognized as the "young lady's boudoir." But the dusty and draped furniture had been rearranged and uncovered, and the apartment bore every sign of present use. Yet, although there was unmistakable evidence of its being used by a person of taste and refinement, he was surprised to see that the garments hanging in an open press were such as were used by negro servants, and that a gaudy handkerchief such as housemaids used for turbans was lying on the pretty silk coverlet. He did not linger over these details, but cast a rapid glance round the room. Then his eyes became fixed on a fanciful writing-desk, which stood by the window. For, in a handsome vase placed on its level top, and drooping on a portfolio below, hung a cluster of the very flowers that Miss Faulkner had carried!

CHAPTER IV

It seemed plain to Brant that the dispatch-box had been conveyed here and opened for security on this desk, and in the hurry of examining the papers the flower had been jostled and the fallen grains of pollen overlooked by the spy. There were one or two freckles of red on the desk, which made this accident appear the more probable. But he was equally struck by another circumstance. The desk stood immediately before the window. As he glanced mechanically from it, he was surprised to see that it commanded an extensive view of the slope below the eminence on which the house stood, even beyond his furthest line of pickets. The vase of flowers, each of which was nearly as large as a magnolia blossom, and striking in color, occupied a central position before it, and no doubt could be quite distinctly seen from a distance. From this circumstance he could not resist the strong impression that this fateful and extraordinary blossom, carried by Miss Faulkner and the mulatto, and so strikingly "in evidence" at the window, was in some way a signal. Obeying an impulse which he was conscious had a half superstitious foundation, he carefully lifted the vase from its position before the window, and placed it on a side table. Then he cautiously slipped from the room.

But he could not easily shake off the perplexity which the occurrence had caused, although he was satisfied that it was

Bret Harte

fraught with no military or strategic danger to his command, and that the unknown spy had obtained no information whatever. Yet he was forced to admit to himself that he was more concerned in his attempts to justify the conduct of Miss Faulkner with this later revelation. It was quite possible that the dispatch-box had been purloined by some one else during her absence from the house, as the presence of the mulatto servant in his room would have been less suspicious than hers. There was really little evidence to connect Miss Faulkner with the actual outrage,—rather might not the real spy have taken advantage of her visit here, to throw suspicion upon her? He remembered her singular manner,— the strange inconsistency with which she had forced this flower upon him. She would hardly have done so had she been conscious of its having so serious an import. Yet, what was the secret of her manifest agitation? A sudden inspiration flashed across his mind; a smile came upon his lips. She was in love! The enemy's line contained some sighing Strephon of a young subaltern with whom she was in communication, and for whom she had undertaken this quest. The flower was their language of correspondence, no doubt. It explained also the young girl's animosity against the younger officers,—his adversaries; against himself,—their commander. He had previously wondered why, if she were indeed a spy, she had not chosen, upon some equally specious order from Washington, the headquarters of the division commander, whose secrets were more valuable. This was explained by the fact that she was nearer the lines and her lover in her present abode. He had no idea that he was making excuses for her,—he believed himself only just. The recollection of what she had said of the power of love, albeit it had hurt him cruelly at the time, was now clearer to him, and even seemed to mitigate her offense. She would be here but a day or two longer; he could afford to wait without interrogating her.

But as to the real intruder, spy or thief,—that was another affair, and quickly settled. He gave an order to the officer of the day peremptorily forbidding the entrance of alien servants or slaves within the precincts of the headquarters. Any one thus trespassing was to be brought before him. The officer looked surprised, he even fancied disappointed. The graces of the mulatto woman's figure had evidently not been thrown away upon his subalterns.

An hour or two later, when he was mounting his horse for a round of inspection, he was surprised to see Miss Faulkner, accompanied by the mulatto woman, running hurriedly to the house. He had forgotten his late order until he saw the latter halted by the sentries, but the young girl came flying on, regardless of her companion. Her skirt was held in one hand, her straw hat had fallen back in her flight, and was caught only by a ribbon around her swelling throat, and her loosened hair lay in a black rippled loop on one shoulder. For an instant Brant thought that she was seeking him in indignation at his order, but a second look at her set face, eager eyes, and parted scarlet lips, showed him that she had not even noticed him in the concentration of her purpose. She swept by him into the hall, he heard the swish of her skirt and rapid feet on the stairs,—she was gone. What had happened, or was this another of her moods?

But he was called to himself by the apparition of a corporal standing before him, with the mulatto woman,—the first capture under his order. She was tall, well-formed, but unmistakably showing the negro type, even in her small features. Her black eyes were excited, but unintelligent; her manner dogged, but with the obstinacy of half-conscious stupidity. Brant felt not only disappointed, but had a singular impression that she was not the same woman that he had first seen. Yet there was the tall, graceful figure, the dark profile, and the turbaned head that he had once followed down the

Bret Harte

passage by his room.

Her story was as stupidly simple. She had known "Missy" from a chile! She had just traipsed over to see her that afternoon; they were walking together when the sojers stopped her. She had never been stopped before, even by "the patter rollers."* Her old massa (Manly) had gib leaf to go see Miss Tilly, and hadn't said nuffin about no "orders."

* i. e., patrols,—a civic home-guard in the South that kept surveillance of slaves.

More annoyed than he cared to confess, Brant briefly dismissed her with a warning. As he cantered down the slope the view of the distant pickets recalled the window in the wing, and he turned in his saddle to look at it. There it was— the largest and most dominant window in that part of the building—and within it, a distinct and vivid object almost filling the opening, was the vase of flowers, which he had a few hours ago removed, RESTORED TO ITS ORIGINAL POSITION! He smiled. The hurried entrance and consternation of Miss Faulkner were now fully explained. He had interrupted some impassioned message, perhaps even countermanded some affectionate rendezvous beyond the lines. And it seemed to settle the fact that it was she who had done the signaling! But would not this also make her cognizant of the taking of the dispatch-box? He reflected, however, that the room was apparently occupied by the mulatto woman—he remembered the calico dresses and turban on the bed—and it was possible that Miss Faulkner had only visited it for the purpose of signaling to her lover. Although this circumstance did not tend to make his mind easier, it was, however, presently diverted by a new arrival and a strange recognition.

As he rode through the camp a group of officers congregated

before a large mess tent appeared to be highly amused by the conversation—half monologue and half harangue of a singular-looking individual who stood in the centre. He wore a "slouch" hat, to the band of which he had imparted a military air by the addition of a gold cord, but the brim was caught up at the side in a peculiarly theatrical and highly artificial fashion. A heavy cavalry sabre depended from a broad-buckled belt under his black frock coat, with the addition of two revolvers—minus their holsters—stuck on either side of the buckle, after the style of a stage smuggler. A pair of long enameled leather riding boots, with the tops turned deeply over, as if they had once done duty for the representative of a cavalier, completed his extraordinary equipment. The group were so absorbed in him that they did not perceive the approach of their chief and his orderly; and Brant, with a sign to the latter, halted only a few paces from this central figure. His speech was a singular mingling of high-flown and exalted epithets, with inexact pronunciation and occasional lapses of Western slang.

"Well, I ain't purtendin' to any stratutegical smartness, and I didn't gradooate at West Point as one of those Apocryphal Engineers; I don't do much talking about 'flank' movements or 'recognizances in force' or 'Ekellon skirmishing,' but when it comes down to square Ingin fightin', I reckon I kin have my say. There are men who don't know the Army Contractor," he added darkly, "who mebbe have heard of 'Red Jim.' I don't mention names, gentlemen, but only the other day a man that you all know says to me, 'If I only knew what you do about scoutin' I wouldn't be wanting for information as I do.' I ain't goin' to say who it was, or break any confidences between gentlemen by saying how many stars he had on his shoulder strap; but he was a man who knew what he was saying. And I say agin, gentlemen, that the curse of the Northern Army is the want of proper scoutin'. What was it caused Bull's Run?—Want o' scoutin'.

What was it rolled up Pope?—Want o' scoutin'. What caused the slaughter at the Wilderness?—Want o' scoutin'—Ingin scoutin'! Why, only the other day, gentlemen, I was approached to know what I'd take to organize a scoutin' force. And what did I say?—'No, General; it ain't because I represent one of the largest Army Beef Contracts in this country,' says I. 'It ain't because I belong, so to speak, to the "Sinews of War;" but because I'd want about ten thousand trained Ingins from the Reservations!' And the regular West Point, high-toned, scientific inkybus that weighs so heavily on our army don't see it—and won't have it! Then Sherman, he sez to me"—

But here a roar of laughter interrupted him, and in the cross fire of sarcastic interrogations that began Brant saw, with relief, a chance of escape. For in the voice, manner, and, above all, the characteristic temperament of the stranger, he had recognized his old playmate and the husband of Susy,— the redoubtable Jim Hooker! There was no mistaking that gloomy audacity; that mysterious significance; that magnificent lying. But even at that moment Clarence Brant's heart had gone out, with all his old loyalty of feeling, towards his old companion. He knew that a public recognition of him then and there would plunge Hooker into confusion; he felt keenly the ironical plaudits and laughter of his officers over the manifest weakness and vanity of the ex-teamster, ex-rancher, ex-actor, and husband of his old girl sweetheart, and would have spared him the knowledge that he had overheard it. Turning hastily to the orderly, he bade him bring the stranger to his headquarters, and rode away unperceived.

He had heard enough, however, to account for his presence there, and the singular chance that had brought them again together. He was evidently one of those large civil contractors of supplies whom the Government was obliged to employ, who visited the camp half officially, and whom the army alternately depended upon and abused. Brant had dealt with his underlings in the Commissariat, and even now remembered that he had heard he was coming, but had overlooked the significance of his name. But how he came to leave his theatrical profession, how he had attained a position which implied a command of considerable capital— for many of the contractors had already amassed large fortunes—and what had become of Susy and her ambitions in this radical change of circumstances, were things still to be learned. In his own changed conditions he had seldom thought of her; it was with a strange feeling of irritation and half responsibility that he now recalled their last interview and the emotion to which he had yielded.

He had not long to wait. He had scarcely regained the quarters at his own private office before he heard the step of the orderly upon the veranda and the trailing clank of Hooker's sabre. He did not know, however, that Hooker, without recognizing his name, had received the message as a personal tribute, and had left his sarcastic companions triumphantly, with the air of going to a confidential interview, to which his well-known military criticism had entitled him. It was with a bearing of gloomy importance and his characteristic, sullen, sidelong glance that he entered the apartment and did not look up until Brant had signaled the orderly to withdraw, and closed the door behind him. And then he recognized his old boyish companion—the preferred favorite of fortune!

For a moment he gasped with astonishment. For a moment gloomy incredulity, suspicion, delight, pride, admiration, even affection, struggled for mastery in his sullen, staring eyes and open, twitching mouth. For here was Clarence Brant, handsomer than ever, more superior than ever, in the majesty of uniform and authority which fitted him—the younger man—by reason of his four years of active service, with the careless ease and bearing of the veteran! Here was the hero whose name was already so famous that the mere coincidence of it with that of the modest civilian he had known would have struck him as preposterous. Yet here he was—supreme, and dazzling—surrounded by the pomp and circumstance of war—into whose reserved presence he, Jim Hooker, had been ushered with the formality of challenge, saluting, and presented bayonets!

Luckily, Brant had taken advantage of his first gratified ejaculation to shake him warmly by the hand, and then, with both hands laid familiarly on his shoulder, force him down into a chair. Luckily, for by that time Jim Hooker had, with characteristic gloominess, found time to taste the pangs of envy—an envy the more keen since, in spite of his success as a peaceful contractor, he had always secretly longed for military display and distinction. He looked at the man who had achieved it, as he firmly believed, by sheer luck and accident, and his eyes darkened. Then, with characteristic weakness and vanity, he began to resist his first impressions of Clarence's superiority, and to air his own importance. He leaned heavily back in the chair in which he had been thus genially forced, drew off his gauntlet and attempted to thrust it through his belt, as he had seen Brant do, but failed on account of his pistols already occupying that position, dropped it, got his sword between his legs in attempting to pick it up, and then leaned back again, with half-closed eyes serenely indifferent of his old companion's smiling face.

"I reckon," he began slowly, with a slightly patronizing air, "that we'd have met, sooner or later, at Washington, or at Grant's headquarters, for Hooker, Meacham & Co. go everywhere, and are about as well known as major-generals, to say nothin'," he went on, with a sidelong glance at Brant's shoulder-straps, "of brigadiers; and it's rather strange—only, of course, you're kind of fresh in the service—that you ain't heard of me afore."

"But I'm very glad to hear of you now, Jim," said Brant, smiling, "and from your own lips—which I am also delighted to find," he added mischievously, "are still as frankly communicative on that topic as of old. But I congratulate you, old fellow, on your good fortune. When did you leave the stage?"

Mr. Hooker frowned slightly.

"I never was really on the stage, you know," he said, waving his hand with assumed negligence. "Only went on to please my wife. Mrs. Hooker wouldn't act with vulgar professionals, don't you see! I was really manager most of the time, and lessee of the theatre. Went East when the war broke out, to offer my sword and knowledge of Ingin fightin' to Uncle Sam! Drifted into a big pork contract at St. Louis, with Fremont. Been at it ever since. Offered a commission in the reg'lar service lots o' times. Refused."

"Why?" asked Brant demurely.

"Too much West Point starch around to suit ME," returned Hooker darkly. "And too many spies!"

"Spies?" echoed Brant abstractedly, with a momentary reminiscence of Miss Faulkner.

"Yes, spies," continued Hooker, with dogged mystery. "One half of Washington is watching t'other half, and, from the President's wife down, most of the women are secesh!"

Brant suddenly fixed his keen eyes on his guest. But the next moment he reflected that this was only Jim Hooker's usual speech, and possessed no ulterior significance. He smiled again, and said, more gently,—

"And how is Mrs. Hooker?"

Mr. Hooker fixed his eyes on the ceiling, rose, and pretended to look out of the window; then, taking his seat again by the table, as if fronting an imaginary audience, and pulling slowly at his gauntlets after the usual theatrical indication of perfect sangfroid, said,—

"There ain't any!"

"Good heavens!" said Brant, with genuine emotion. "I beg your pardon. Really, I"—

"Mrs. Hooker and me are divorced," continued Hooker, slightly changing his attitude, and leaning heavily on his sabre, with his eyes still on his fanciful audience. "There was, you understand"—lightly tossing his gauntlet aside—"incompatibility of temper—and—we—parted! Ha!"

He uttered a low, bitter, scornful laugh, which, however, produced the distinct impression in Brant's mind that up to that moment he had never had the slightest feeling in the matter whatever.

"You seemed to be on such good terms with each other!" murmured Brant vaguely.

"Seemed!" said Hooker bitterly, glancing sardonically at an ideal second row in the pit before him, "yes—seemed! There were other differences, social and political. You understand that; you have suffered, too." He reached out his hand and pressed Brant's, in heavy effusiveness. "But," he continued haughtily, lightly tossing his glove again, "we are also men of the world; we let that pass."

And it was possible that he found the strain of his present attitude too great, for he changed to an easier position.

"But," said Brant curiously, "I always thought that Mrs. Hooker was intensely Union and Northern?"

"Put on!" said Hooker, in his natural voice.

"But you remember the incident of the flag?" persisted Brant.

"Mrs. Hooker was always an actress," said Hooker significantly. "But," he added cheerfully, "Mrs. Hooker is now the wife of Senator Boompointer, one of the wealthiest and most powerful Republicans in Washington—carries the patronage of the whole West in his vest pocket."

"Yet, if she is not a Republican, why did she"—began Brant.

"For a purpose," replied Hooker darkly. "But," he added again, with greater cheerfulness, "she belongs to the very elite of Washington society. Goes to all the foreign ambassadors' balls, and is a power at the White House. Her picture is in all the first-class illustrated papers."

The singular but unmistakable pride of the man in the importance of the wife from whom he was divorced, and for whom he did not care, would have offended Brant's delicacy, or at least have excited his ridicule, but for the reason that he was more deeply stung by Hooker's allusion to his own wife and his degrading similitude of their two conditions. But he dismissed the former as part of Hooker's invincible and still boyish extravagance, and the latter as part of his equally characteristic assumption. Perhaps he was conscious, too, notwithstanding the lapse of years and the condonation of separation and forgetfulness, that he deserved little delicacy from the hands of Susy's husband. Nevertheless, he dreaded

Bret Harte

to hear him speak again of her; and the fear was realized in a question.

"Does she know you are here?"

"Who?" said Brant curtly.

"Your wife. That is—I reckon she's your wife still, eh?"

"Yes; but I do not know what she knows," returned Brant quietly. He had regained his self-composure.

"Susy,—Mrs. Senator Boompointer, that is,"—said Hooker, with an apparent dignity in his late wife's new title, "allowed that she'd gone abroad on a secret mission from the Southern Confederacy to them crowned heads over there. She was good at ropin' men in, you know. Anyhow, Susy, afore she was Mrs. Boompointer, was dead set on findin' out where she was, but never could. She seemed to drop out of sight a year ago. Some said one thing, and some said another. But you can bet your bottom dollar that Mrs. Senator Boompointer, who knows how to pull all the wires in Washington, will know, if any one does."

"But is Mrs. Boompointer really disaffected, and a Southern sympathizer?" said Brant, "or is it only caprice or fashion?"

While speaking he had risen, with a half-abstracted face, and had gone to the window, where he stood in a listening attitude. Presently he opened the window, and stepped outside. Hooker wonderingly followed him. One or two officers had already stepped out of their rooms, and were standing upon the veranda; another had halted in the path. Then one quickly re-entered the house, reappeared with his cap and sword in his hand, and ran lightly toward the guard-house. A slight crackling noise seemed to come from beyond the garden wall.

"What's up?" said Hooker, with staring eyes.

"Picket firing!"

The crackling suddenly became a long rattle. Brant re-entered the room, and picked up his hat.

"You'll excuse me for a few moments."

A faint sound, soft yet full, and not unlike a bursting bubble, made the house appear to leap elastically, like the rebound of a rubber ball.

"What's that?" gasped Hooker.

"Cannon, out of range!"

CHAPTER V

In another instant bugles were ringing through the camp, with the hurrying hoofs of mounted officers and the trampling of forming men. The house itself was almost deserted. Although the single cannon-shot had been enough to show that it was no mere skirmishing of pickets, Brant still did not believe in any serious attack of the enemy. His position, as in the previous engagement, had no strategic importance to them; they were no doubt only making a feint against it to conceal some advance upon the centre of the army two miles away. Satisfied that he was in easy supporting distance of his division commander, he extended his line along the ridge, ready to fall back in that direction, while retarding their advance and masking the position of his own chief. He gave a few orders necessary to the probable abandonment of the house, and then returned to it. Shot and shell were already dropping in the field below. A thin ridge of blue haze showed the line of skirmish fire. A small conical, white cloud, like a bursting cotton-pod, revealed an open battery in the willow-fringed meadow. Yet the pastoral peacefulness of the house was unchanged. The afternoon sun lay softly on its deep verandas; the pot pourri incense of fallen rose-leaves haunted it still.

He entered his room through the French window on the veranda, when the door leading from the passage was suddenly flung open, and Miss Faulkner swept quickly inside, closed the door behind her, and leaned back against it, panting and breathless.

Clarence was startled, and for a moment ashamed. He had suddenly realized that in the excitement he had entirely forgotten her and the dangers to which she might be exposed. She had probably heard the firing, her womanly fears had been awakened; she had come to him for protection. But as he turned towards her with a reassuring smile, he was shocked to see that her agitation and pallor were far beyond any physical cause. She motioned him desperately to shut the window by which he had entered, and said, with white lips,—

"I must speak with you alone!"

"Certainly. But there is no immediate danger to you even here—and I can soon put you beyond the reach of any possible harm."

"Harm—to me! God! if it were only that!"

He stared at her uneasily.

"Listen," she said gaspingly, "listen to me! Then hate, despise me—kill me if you will. For you are betrayed and ruined—cut off and surrounded! It has been helped on by me, but I swear to you the blow did not come from MY hand. I would have saved you. God only knows how it happened—it was Fate!"

In an instant Brant saw the whole truth instinctively and clearly. But with the revelation came the usual calmness and perfect self-possession which never yet had failed him in any emergency. With the sound of the increasing cannonade and its shifting position made clearer to his ears, the view of his whole threatened position spread out like a map before his eyes, the swift calculation of the time his men could hold the ridge in his mind—even a hurried estimate of the precious moments he could give to the wretched woman before him— he even then, gravely and gently, led her to a chair and said in a calm voice,—

"That is not enough! Speak slowly, plainly. I must know everything. How and in what way have you betrayed me?"

She looked at him imploringly—reassured, yet awed by his gentleness.

"You won't believe me; you cannot believe me! for I do not even know. I have taken and exchanged letters—whose contents I never saw—between the Confederates and a spy who comes to this house, but who is far away by this time. I did it because I thought you hated and despised me because I thought it was my duty to help my cause—because you said it was 'war' between us—but I never spied on you. I swear it."

"Then how do you know of this attack?" he said calmly.

She brightened, half timidly, half hopefully.

"There is a window in the wing of this house that overlooks the slope near the Confederate lines. There was a signal placed in it—not by me—but I know it meant that as long as it was there the plot, whatever it was, was not ripe, and that no attack would be made on you as long as it was visible. That much I know,—that much the spy had to tell me, for we both had to guard that room in turns. I wanted to keep this dreadful thing off—until"—her voice trembled, "until," she added hurriedly, seeing his calm eyes were reading her very soul, "until I went away—and for that purpose I withheld some of the letters that were given me. But this morning, while I was away from the house, I looked back and saw that the signal was no longer there. Some one had changed it. I ran back, but I was too late—God help me!—as you see."

The truth flashed upon Brant. It was his own hand that had precipitated the attack. But a larger truth came to him now, like a dazzling inspiration. If he had thus precipitated the attack before they were ready, there was a chance that it was imperfect, and there was still hope. But there was no trace of this visible in his face as he fixed his eyes calmly on hers, although his pulses were halting in expectancy as he said—

"Then the spy had suspected you, and changed it."

"Oh, no," she said eagerly, "for the spy was with me and was frightened too. We both ran back together—you remember—she was stopped by the patrol!"

She checked herself suddenly, but too late. Her cheeks blazed, her head sank, with the foolish identification of the spy into which her eagerness had betrayed her.

But Brant appeared not to notice it. He was, in fact, puzzling his brain to conceive what information the stupid mulatto woman could have obtained here. His strength, his position was no secret to the enemy—there was nothing to gain from him. She must have been, like the trembling, eager woman before him, a mere tool of others.

"Did this woman live here?" he said.

"No," she said. "She lived with the Manlys, but had friends whom she visited at your general's headquarters."

With difficulty Brant suppressed a start. It was clear to him now. The information had been obtained at the division headquarters, and passed through his camp as being nearest the Confederate lines. But what was the information—and what movement had he precipitated? It was clear that this woman did not know. He looked at her keenly. A sudden explosion shook the house,—a drift of smoke passed the window,—a shell had burst in the garden.

She had been gazing at him despairingly, wistfully—but did not blanch or start.

An idea took possession of him. He approached her, and took her cold hand. A half-smile parted her pale lips.

"You have courage—you have devotion," he said gravely. "I believe you regret the step you have taken. If you could undo what you have done, even at peril to yourself, dare you do it?"

"Yes," she said breathlessly.

"You are known to the enemy. If I am surrounded, you could pass through their lines unquestioned?"

"Yes," she said eagerly.

"A note from me would pass you again through the pickets of our headquarters. But you would bear a note to the general that no eyes but his must see. It would not implicate you or yours; would only be a word of warning."

"And you," she said quickly, "would be saved! They would come to your assistance! You would not then be taken?"

He smiled gently.

"Perhaps—who knows!"

He sat down and wrote hurriedly.

"This," he said, handing her a slip of paper, "is a pass. You will use it beyond your own lines. This note," he continued, handing her a sealed envelope, "is for the general. No one else must see it or know of it—not even your lover, should you meet him!"

"My lover!" she said indignantly, with a flash of her old savagery; "what do you mean? I have no lover!"

Brant glanced at her flushed face.

"I thought," he said quietly, "that there was some one you cared for in yonder lines—some one you wrote to. It would have been an excuse"—

He stopped, as her face paled again, and her hands dropped heavily at her side.

"Good God!—you thought that, too! You thought that I would sacrifice you for another man!"

"Pardon me," said Brant quickly. "I was foolish. But whether your lover is a man or a cause, you have shown a woman's devotion. And, in repairing your fault, you are showing more than a woman's courage now."

To his surprise, the color had again mounted her pretty cheeks, and even a flash of mischief shone in her blue eyes.

"It would have been an excuse," she murmured, "yes—to save a man, surely!" Then she said quickly, "I will go. At once! I am ready!"

"One moment," he said gravely. "Although this pass and an

escort insure your probable safe conduct, this is 'war' and danger! You are still a spy! Are you ready to go?"

"I am," she said proudly, tossing back a braid of her fallen hair. Yet a moment after she hesitated. Then she said, in a lower voice, "Are you ready to forgive?"

"In either case," he said, touched by her manner; "and God speed you!"

He extended his hand, and left a slight pressure on her cold fingers. But they slipped quickly from his grasp, and she turned away with a heightened color.

He stepped to the door. One or two aides-de-camp, withheld by his order against intrusion, were waiting eagerly with reports. The horse of a mounted field officer was pawing the garden turf. The officers stared at the young girl.

"Take Miss Faulkner, with a flag, to some safe point of the enemy's line. She is a non-combatant of their own, and will receive their protection."

He had scarcely exchanged a dozen words with the aides-de-camp before the field officer hurriedly entered. Taking Brant aside, he said quickly,—

"Pardon me, General; but there is a strong feeling among the men that this attack is the result of some information obtained by the enemy. You must know that the woman you have just given a safeguard to is suspected, and the men are indignant."

"The more reason why she should be conveyed beyond any consequences of their folly, Major," said Brant frigidly, "and I look to you for her safe convoy. There is nothing in this attack to show that the enemy has received any information regarding us. But I would suggest that it would be better to see that my orders are carried out regarding the slaves and non-combatants who are passing our lines from divisional headquarters, where valuable information may be obtained, than in the surveillance of a testy and outspoken girl."

An angry flush crossed the major's cheek as he saluted and fell back, and Brant turned to the aide-de-camp. The news was grave. The column of the enemy was moving against the ridge—it was no longer possible to hold it—and the brigade was cut off from its communication with the divisional headquarters, although as yet no combined movement was made against it. Brant's secret fears that it was an intended impact against the centre were confirmed. Would his communication to the divisional commander pass through the attacking column in time?

Yet one thing puzzled him. The enemy, after forcing his flank, had shown no disposition, even with their over-whelming force, to turn aside and crush him. He could easily have fallen back, when it was possible to hold the ridge no longer, without pursuit. His other flank and rear were not threatened, as they might have been, by the division of so large an attacking column, which was moving steadily on towards the ridge. It was this fact that seemed to show a failure or imperfection in the enemy's plan. It was possible that his precipitation of the attack by the changed signal had been the cause of it. Doubtless some provision had been made to attack him in flank and rear, but in the unexpected hurry of the onset it had to be abandoned. He could still save himself, as his officers knew; but his conviction that he might yet be able to support his divisional commander by holding his position doggedly, but coolly awaiting his opportunity, was strong. More than that, it was his tempera-ment and instinct.

Harrying them in flank and rear, contesting the ground inch by inch, and holding his own against the artillery sent to dislodge him, or the outriding cavalry that, circling round, swept through his open ranks, he saw his files melt away beside this steady current without flinching.

CHAPTER VI

Yet all along the fateful ridge—now obscured and confused with thin crossing smoke-drifts from file-firing, like partly rubbed-out slate-pencil marks; or else, when cleared of those drifts, presenting only an indistinguishable map of zigzag lines of straggling wagons and horses, unintelligible to any eye but his—the singular magnetism of the chief was felt everywhere: whether it was shown in the quick closing in of resistance to some sharper onset of the enemy or the more dogged stand of inaction under fire, his power was always dominant. A word or two of comprehensive direction sent through an aide-de-camp, or the sudden relief of his dark, watchful, composed face uplifted above a line of bayonets, never failed in their magic. Like all born leaders, he seemed in these emergencies to hold a charmed life—infecting his followers with a like disbelief in death; men dropped to right and left of him with serene assurance in their ghastly faces or a cry of life and confidence in their last gasp. Stragglers fell in and closed up under his passing glance; a hopeless, inextricable wrangle around an overturned caisson, at a turn of the road, resolved itself into an orderly, quiet, deliberate clearing away of the impediment before the significant waiting of that dark, silent horseman.

Yet under this imperturbable mask he was keenly conscious of everything; in that apparent concentration there was a

Bret Harte

sharpening of all his senses and his impressibility: he saw the first trace of doubt or alarm in the face of a subaltern to whom he was giving an order; the first touch of sluggishness in a re-forming line; the more significant clumsiness of a living evolution that he knew was clogged by the dead bodies of comrades; the ominous silence of a breastwork; the awful inertia of some rigidly kneeling files beyond, which still kept their form but never would move again; the melting away of skirmish points; the sudden gaps here and there; the sickening incurving of what a moment before had been a straight line—all these he saw in all their fatal significance. But even at this moment, coming upon a hasty barricade of overset commissary wagons, he stopped to glance at a familiar figure he had seen but an hour ago, who now seemed to be commanding a group of collected stragglers and camp followers. Mounted on a wheel, with a revolver in each hand and a bowie knife between his teeth—theatrical even in his paroxysm of undoubted courage—glared Jim Hooker. And Clarence Brant, with the whole responsibility of the field on his shoulders, even at that desperate moment, found himself recalling a vivid picture of the actor Hooker personating the character of "Red Dick" in "Rosalie, the Prairie Flower," as he had seen him in a California theatre five years before.

It wanted still an hour of the darkness that would probably close the fight of that day. Could he hold out, keeping his offensive position so long? A hasty council with his officers showed him that the weakness of their position had already infected them. They reminded him that his line of retreat was still open—that in the course of the night the enemy, although still pressing towards the division centre, might yet turn and outflank him—or that their strangely delayed supports might come up before morning. Brant's glass, however, remained fixed on the main column, still pursuing its way along the ridge. It struck him suddenly, however, that the steady current had stopped, spread out along the crest on both sides, and was now at right angles with its previous course. There had been a check! The next moment the thunder of guns along the whole horizon, and the rising cloud of smoke, revealed a line of battle. The division centre was engaged. The opportunity he had longed for had come—the desperate chance to throw himself on their rear and cut his way through to the division—but it had come too late! He looked at his shattered ranks—scarce a regiment remained. Even as a demonstration, the attack would fail against the enemy's superior numbers. Nothing clearly was left to him now but to remain where he was—within supporting distance, and await the issue of the fight beyond. He was putting up his glass, when the dull boom of cannon in the extreme western limit of the horizon attracted his attention. By the still gleaming sky he could see a long gray line stealing up from the valley from the distant rear of the headquarters to join the main column. They were the missing supports! His heart leaped. He held the key of the mystery now. The one imperfect detail of the enemy's plan was before him. The supports, coming later from the west, had only seen the second signal from the window—when Miss Faulkner had replaced the vase—and had avoided his position. It was impossible to limit the effect of this blunder. If the young girl who had thus saved him had reached the division commander with his message in time, he might be forewarned, and even profit by it. His own position would be less precarious, as the enemy, already engaged in front, would be unable to recover their position in the rear and correct the blunder. The bulk of their column had already streamed past him. If defeated, there was always the danger that it might be rolled back upon him—but he conjectured that the division commander would attempt to prevent the junction of the supports with the main column by breaking between them, crowding them from the ridge, and joining him. As the last stragglers of the rear guard swept by, Brant's bugles were already recalling the skirmishers. He redoubled his pickets, and resolved to wait and watch.

And there was the more painful duty of looking after the wounded and the dead. The larger rooms of the headquarters had already been used as a hospital. Passing from cot to cot, recognizing in the faces now drawn with agony, or staring in vacant unconsciousness, the features that he had seen only a few hours before flushed with enthusiasm and excitement, something of his old doubting, questioning nature returned. Was there no way but this? How far was HE—moving among them unscathed and uninjured—responsible?

And if not he—who then? His mind went back bitterly to the old days of the conspiracy—to the inception of that struggle which was bearing such ghastly fruit. He thought of his traitorous wife, until he felt his cheeks tingle, and he was fain to avert his eyes from those of his prostrate comrades, in a strange fear that, with the clairvoyance of dying men, they should read his secret.

It was past midnight when, without undressing, he threw himself upon his bed in the little convent-like cell to snatch a few moments of sleep. Its spotless, peaceful walls and draperies affected him strangely, as if he had brought into its immaculate serenity the sanguine stain of war. He was awakened suddenly from a deep slumber by an indefinite sense of alarm. His first thought was that he had been summoned to repel an attack. He sat up and listened; everything was silent except the measured tread of the sentry on the gravel walk below. But the door was open. He sprang to his feet and slipped into the gallery in time to see the tall figure of a woman glide before the last moonlit window at its farthest end. He could not see her face—but the characteristic turbaned head of the negro race was plainly visible.

He did not care to follow her or even to alarm the guard. If it were the spy or one of her emissaries, she was powerless now to do any harm, and under his late orders and the rigorous vigilance of his sentinels she could not leave the lines—or, indeed, the house. She probably knew this as well as he did; it was, therefore, no doubt only an accidental intrusion of one of the servants. He re-entered the room, and stood for a few moments by the window, looking over the moonlit ridge. The sounds of distant cannon had long since ceased. Wide awake, and refreshed by the keen morning air, which alone of all created things seemed to have shaken the burden of the dreadful yesterday from its dewy wings, he turned away and lit a candle on the table. As he was rebuckling his sword belt he saw a piece of paper lying on the foot of the bed from which he had just risen. Taking it to the candle, he read in a roughly scrawled hand:

"You are asleep when you should be on the march. You have no time to lose. Before daybreak the supports of the column you have been foolishly resisting will be upon you.—From one who would save YOU, but hates your cause."

A smile of scorn passed his lips. The handwriting was unknown and evidently disguised. The purport of the message had not alarmed him; but suddenly a suspicion flashed upon him—that it came from Miss Faulkner! She had failed in her attempt to pass through the enemy's lines—or she had never tried to. She had deceived him—or had thought better of her chivalrous impulse, and now sought to mitigate her second treachery by this second warning. And he had let her messenger escape him!

He hurriedly descended the stairs. The sound of voices was approaching him. He halted, and recognized the faces of the brigade surgeon and one of his aides-de-camp.

Bret Harte

"We were hesitating whether to disturb you, general, but it may be an affair of some importance. Under your orders a negro woman was just now challenged stealing out of the lines. Attempting to escape, she was chased, there was a struggle and scramble over the wall, and she fell, striking her head. She was brought into the guardhouse unconscious."

"Very good. I will see her," said Brant, with a feeling of relief.

"One moment, general. We thought you would perhaps prefer to see her alone," said the surgeon, "for when I endeavored to bring her to, and was sponging her face and head to discover her injuries, her color came off! She was a white woman—stained and disguised as a mulatto."

For an instant Brant's heart sank. It was Miss Faulkner.

"Did you recognize her?" he said, glancing from the one to the other. "Have you seen her here before?"

"No, sir," replied the aide-de-camp. "But she seemed to be quite a superior woman—a lady, I should say."

Brant breathed more freely.

"Where is she now?" he asked.

"In the guardhouse. We thought it better not to bring her into hospital, among the men, until we had your orders."

"You have done well," returned Brant gravely. "And you will keep this to yourselves for the present; but see that she is brought here quietly and with as little publicity as possible. Put her in my room above, which I give up to her and any necessary attendant. But you will look carefully after her, doctor,"—he turned to the surgeon,—"and when she recovers consciousness let me know."

He moved away. Although attaching little importance to the mysterious message, whether sent by Miss Faulkner or emanating from the stranger herself, which, he reasoned, was based only upon a knowledge of the original plan of attack, he nevertheless quickly dispatched a small scouting party in the direction from which the attack might come, with orders to fall back and report at once. With a certain half irony of recollection he had selected Jim Hooker to accompany the party as a volunteer. This done, he returned to the gallery. The surgeon met him at the door.

"The indications of concussion are passing away," he said, "but she seems to be suffering from the exhaustion following some great nervous excitement. You may go in—she may rally from it at any moment."

With the artificial step and mysterious hush of the ordinary visitor to a sick bed, Brant entered the room. But some instinct greater than this common expression of humanity held him suddenly in awe. The room seemed no longer his— it had slipped back into that austere conventual privacy which had first impressed him. Yet he hesitated; another strange suggestion—it seemed almost a vague recollection— overcame him like some lingering perfume, far off and pathetic, in its dying familiarity. He turned his eyes almost timidly towards the bed. The coverlet was drawn up near the throat of the figure to replace the striped cotton gown stained with blood and dust, which had been hurriedly torn off and thrown on a chair. The pale face, cleansed of blood and disguising color, the long hair, still damp from the surgeon's sponge, lay rigidly back on the pillow. Suddenly this man of steady nerve uttered a faint cry, and, with a face as white as the upturned one before him, fell on his knees beside the bed.

Bret Harte

For the face that lay there was his wife's!

Yes, hers! But the beautiful hair that she had gloried in—the hair that in his youth he had thought had once fallen like a benediction on his shoulder—was streaked with gray along the blue-veined hollows of the temples; the orbits of those clear eyes, beneath their delicately arched brows, were ringed with days of suffering; only the clear-cut profile, even to the delicate imperiousness of lips and nostril, was still there in all its beauty. The coverlet had slipped from her shoulder; its familiar cold contour startled him. He remembered how, in their early married days, he had felt the sanctity of that Diana-like revelation, and the still nymph-like austerity which clung to this strange, childless woman. He even fancied that he breathed again the subtle characteristic perfume of the laces, embroideries, and delicate enwrappings in her chamber at Robles. Perhaps it was the intensity of his gaze—perhaps it was the magnetism of his presence—but her lips parted with a half sigh, half moan. Her head, although her eyes were still closed, turned on the pillow instinctively towards him. He rose from his knees. Her eyes opened slowly. As the first glare of wonderment cleared from them, they met him—in the old antagonism of spirit. Yet her first gesture was a pathetic feminine movement with both hands to arrange her straggling hair. It brought her white fingers, cleaned of their disguising stains, as a sudden revelation to her of what had happened; she instantly slipped them back under the coverlet again. Brant did not speak, but with folded arms stood gazing upon her. And it was her voice that first broke the silence.

"You have recognized me? Well, I suppose you know all," she said, with a weak half-defiance.

He bowed his head. He felt as yet he could not trust his voice, and envied her her own.

"I may sit up, mayn't I?" She managed, by sheer force of will, to struggle to a sitting posture. Then, as the coverlet slipped from the bare shoulder, she said, as she drew it, with a shiver of disgust, around her again,—

"I forgot that you strip women, you Northern soldiers! But I forgot, too," she added, with a sarcastic smile, "that you are also my husband, and I am in your room."

The contemptuous significance of her speech dispelled the last lingering remnant of Brant's dream. In a voice as dry as her own, he said,—

"I am afraid you will now have to remember only that I am a Northern general, and you a Southern spy."

"So be it," she said gravely. Then impulsively, "But I have not spied on YOU."

Yet, the next moment, she bit her lips as if the expression had unwittingly escaped her; and with a reckless shrug of her shoulders she lay back on her pillow.

"It matters not," said Brant coldly. "You have used this house and those within it to forward your designs. It is not your fault that you found nothing in the dispatch-box you opened."

She stared at him quickly; then shrugged her shoulders again.

"I might have known she was false to me," she said bitterly, "and that you would wheedle her soul away as you have others. Well, she betrayed me! For what?"

A flush passed over Brant's face. But with an effort he

contained himself.

"It was the flower that betrayed you! The flower whose red dust fell in the box when you opened it on the desk by the window in yonder room—the flower that stood in the window as a signal—the flower I myself removed, and so spoiled the miserable plot that your friends concocted."

A look of mingled terror and awe came into her face.

"YOU changed the signal!" she repeated dazedly; then, in a lower voice, "that accounts for it all!" But the next moment she turned again fiercely upon him. "And you mean to tell me that she didn't help you—that she didn't sell me—your wife—to you for—for what was it? A look—a kiss!"

"I mean to say that she did not know the signal was changed, and that she herself restored it to its place. It is no fault of hers nor yours that I am not here a prisoner."

She passed her thin hand dazedly across her forehead.

"I see," she muttered. Then again bursting out passionately, she said—"Fool! you never would have been touched! Do you think that Lee would have gone for you, with higher game in your division commander? No! Those supports were a feint to draw him to your assistance while our main column broke his centre. Yes, you may stare at me, Clarence Brant. You are a good lawyer—they say a dashing fighter, too. I never thought you a coward, even in your irresolution; but you are fighting with men drilled in the art of war and strategy when you were a boy outcast on the plains." She stopped, closed her eyes, and then added, wearily—"But that was yesterday—to-day, who knows? All may be changed. The supports may still attack you. That was why I stopped to write you that note an hour ago, when I believed I should be leaving here for ever. Yes, I did it!" she went on, with half-wearied, half-dogged determination. "You may as well know all. I had arranged to fly. Your pickets were to be drawn by friends of mine, who were waiting for me beyond your lines. Well, I lingered here when I saw you arrive—lingered to write you that note. And—I was too late!"

But Brant had been watching her varying expression, her kindling eye, her strange masculine grasp of military knowledge, her soldierly phraseology, all so new to her, that he scarcely heeded the feminine ending of her speech. It seemed to him no longer the Diana of his youthful fancy, but some Pallas Athene, who now looked up at him from the pillow. He had never before fully believed in her unselfish devotion to the cause until now, when it seemed to have almost unsexed her. In his wildest comprehension of her he had never dreamed her a Joan of Arc, and yet hers was the face which might have confronted him, exalted and inspired, on the battlefield itself. He recalled himself with an effort.

"I thank you for your would-be warning," he said more gently, if not so tenderly, "and God knows I wish your flight had been successful. But even your warning is unnecessary, for the supports had already come up; they had followed the second signal, and diverged to engage our division on the left, leaving me alone. And their ruse of drawing our commander to assist me would not have been successful, as I had suspected it, and sent a message to him that I wanted no help."

It was the truth; it was the sole purport of the note he had sent through Miss Faulkner. He would not have disclosed his sacrifice; but so great was the strange domination of this woman still over him, that he felt compelled to assert his superiority. She fixed her eyes upon him.

"And Miss Faulkner took your message?" she said slowly. "Don't deny it! No one else could have passed through our lines; and you gave her a safe conduct through yours. Yes, I might have known it. And this was the creature they sent me for an ally and confidant!"

For an instant Brant felt the sting of this enforced contrast between the two women. But he only said,—

"You forget that I did not know you were the spy, nor do I believe that she suspected you were my wife."

"Why should she?" she said almost fiercely. "I am known among these people only by the name of Benham—my maiden name. Yes!—you can take me out, and shoot me under that name, without disgracing yours. Nobody will know that the Southern spy was the wife of the Northern general! You see, I have thought even of that!"

"And thinking of that," said Brant slowly, "you have put yourself—I will not say in my power, for you are in the power of any man in this camp who may know you, or even hear you speak. Well, let us understand each other plainly. I do not know how great a sacrifice your devotion to your cause demands of you; I do know what it seems to demand of me. Hear me, then! I will do my best to protect you, and get you safely away from here; but, failing that, I tell you plainly that I shall blow out your brains and my own together."

She knew that he would do it. Yet her eyes suddenly beamed with a new and awakening light; she put back her hair again, and half raised herself upon the pillow, to gaze at his dark, set face.

"And as I shall let no other life but ours be periled in this affair," he went on quietly, "and will accompany you myself in some disguise beyond the lines, we will together take the risks—or the bullets of the sentries that may save us both all further trouble. An hour or two more will settle that. Until then your weak condition will excuse you from any disturbance or intrusion here. The mulatto woman you have sometimes personated may be still in this house; I will appoint her to attend you. I suppose you can trust her, for you must personate her again, and escape in her clothes, while she takes your place in this room as my prisoner."

"Clarence!"

Her voice had changed suddenly; it was no longer bitter and stridulous, but low and thrilling as he had heard her call to him that night in the patio of Robles. He turned quickly. She was leaning from the bed—her thin, white hands stretched appealingly towards him.

"Let us go together, Clarence," she said eagerly. "Let us leave this horrible place—these wicked, cruel people—forever. Come with me! Come with me to my people—to my own faith—to my own house—which shall be yours! Come with me to defend it with your good sword, Clarence, against those vile invaders with whom you have nothing in common, and who are the dirt under your feet. Yes, yes! I know it!—I have done you wrong—I have lied to you when I spoke against your skill and power. You are a hero—a born leader of men! I know it! Have I not heard it from the men who have fought against you, and yet admired and understood you, ay, better than your own?—gallant men, Clarence, soldiers bred who did not know what you were to me nor how proud I was of you even while I hated you? Come with me! Think what we would do together—with one faith—one cause—one ambition! Think, Clarence, there is no limit you might not attain! We are no niggards of our rewards and honors—we have no hireling votes to truckle to—we know our friends! Even I—Clarence—I"—there was a strange pathos in the sudden humility that seemed to overcome her— "I have had my reward and known my power. I have been sent abroad, in the confidence of the highest—to the highest. Don't turn from me. I am offering you no bribe, Clarence, only your deserts. Come with me. Leave these curs behind, and live the hero that you are!"

He turned his blazing eyes upon her.

"If you were a man"—he began passionately, then stopped.

"No! I am only a woman and must fight in a woman's way," she interrupted bitterly. "Yes! I intreat, I implore, I wheedle, I flatter, I fawn, I lie! I creep where you stand upright, and pass through doors to which you would not bow. You wear your blazon of honor on your shoulder; I hide mine in a slave's gown. And yet I have worked and striven and suffered! Listen, Clarence," her voice again sank to its appealing minor,—"I know what you men call 'honor,' that which makes you cling to a merely spoken word, or an empty oath. Well, let that pass! I am weary; I have done my share of this work, you have done yours. Let us both fly; let us leave the fight to those who shall come after us, and let us go together to some distant land where the sounds of these guns or the blood of our brothers no longer cry out to us for vengeance! There are those living here—I have met them, Clarence," she went on hurriedly, "who think it wrong to lift up fratricidal hands in the struggle, yet who cannot live under the Northern yoke. They are," her voice hesitated, "good men and women—they are respected—they are"—

"Recreants and slaves, before whom you, spy as you are— stand a queen!" broke in Brant, passionately. He stopped and turned towards the window. After a pause he came back again towards the bed—paused again and then said in a lower voice—"Four years ago, Alice, in the patio of our house at Robles, I might have listened to this proposal, and—I tremble to think—I might have accepted it! I loved you; I was as weak, as selfish, as unreflecting, my life was as purposeless—but for you—as the creatures you speak of. But give me now, at least, the credit of a devotion to my cause equal to your own—a credit which I have never denied you! For the night that you left me, I awoke to a sense of my own worthlessness and degradation—perhaps I have even to thank you for that awakening—and I realized the bitter truth. But that night I found my true vocation—my purpose, my manhood"—

A bitter laugh came from the pillow on which she had languidly thrown herself.

"I believe I left you with Mrs. Hooker—spare me the details."

The blood rushed to Brant's face and then receded as suddenly.

"You left me with Captain Pinckney, who had tempted you, and whom I killed!" he said furiously.

They were both staring savagely at each other. Suddenly he said, "Hush!" and sprang towards the door, as the sound of hurried footsteps echoed along the passage. But he was too late; it was thrown open to the officer of the guard, who appeared, standing on the threshold.

"Two Confederate officers arrested hovering around our pickets. They demand to see you."

Before Brant could interpose, two men in riding cloaks of

Confederate gray stepped into the room with a jaunty and self-confident air.

"Not DEMAND, general," said the foremost, a tall, distinguished-looking man, lifting his hand with a graceful deprecating air. "In fact, too sorry to bother you with an affair of no importance except to ourselves. A bit of after-dinner bravado brought us in contact with your pickets, and, of course, we had to take the consequences. Served us right, and we were lucky not to have got a bullet through us. Gad! I'm afraid my men would have been less discreet! I am Colonel Lagrange, of the 5th Tennessee; my young friend here is Captain Faulkner, of the 1st Kentucky. Some excuse for a youngster like him—none for me! I"—

He stopped, for his eyes suddenly fell upon the bed and its occupant. Both he and his companion started. But to the natural, unaffected dismay of a gentleman who had unwittingly intruded upon a lady's bedchamber, Brant's quick eye saw a more disastrous concern superadded. Colonel Lagrange was quick to recover himself, as they both removed their caps.

"A thousand pardons," he said, hurriedly stepping backwards to the door. "But I hardly need say to a fellow-officer, general, that we had no idea of making so gross an intrusion! We heard some cock-and-bull story of your being occupied—cross-questioning an escaped or escaping nigger—or we should never have forced ourselves upon you."

Brant glanced quickly at his wife. Her face had apparently become rigid on the entrance of the two men; her eyes were coldly fixed upon the ceiling. He bowed formally, and, with a wave of his hand towards the door, said,—

"I will hear your story below, gentleman."

He followed them from the room, stopped to quietly turn the key in the lock, and then motioned them to precede him down the staircase.

Bret Harte

CHAPTER VII

Not a word was exchanged till they had reached the lower landing and Brant's private room. Dismissing his subaltern and orderly with a sign, Brant turned towards his prisoners. The jaunty ease, but not the self-possession, had gone from Lagrange's face; the eyes of Captain Faulkner were fixed on his older companion with a half-humorous look of perplexity.

"I am afraid I can only repeat, general, that our foolhardy freak has put us in collision with your sentries," said Lagrange, with a slight hauteur, that replaced his former jauntiness; "and we were very properly made prisoners. If you will accept my parole, I have no doubt our commander will proceed to exchange a couple of gallant fellows of yours, whom I have had the honor of meeting within our own lines, and whom you must miss probably more than I fear our superiors miss us."

"Whatever brought you here, gentlemen," said Brant drily, "I am glad, for your sakes, that you are in uniform, although it does not, unfortunately, relieve me of an unpleasant duty."

"I don't think I understand you," returned Lagrange, coldly.

"If you had not been in uniform, you would probably have

been shot down as spies, without the trouble of capture," said Brant quietly.

"Do you mean to imply, sir"—began Lagrange sternly.

"I mean to say that the existence of a Confederate spy between this camp and the division headquarters is sufficiently well known to us to justify the strongest action."

"And pray, how can that affect us?" said Lagrange haughtily.

"I need not inform so old a soldier as Colonel Lagrange that the aiding, abetting, and even receiving information from a spy or traitor within one's lines is an equally dangerous service."

"Perhaps you would like to satisfy yourself, General," said Colonel Lagrange, with an ironical laugh. "Pray do not hesitate on account of our uniform. Search us if you like."

"Not on entering my lines, Colonel," replied Brant, with quiet significance.

Lagrange's cheek flushed. But he recovered himself quickly, and with a formal bow said,—

"You will, then, perhaps, let us know your pleasure?"

"My DUTY, Colonel, is to keep you both close prisoners here until I have an opportunity to forward you to the division commander, with a report of the circumstances of your arrest. That I propose to do. How soon I may have that opportunity, or if I am ever to have it," continued Brant, fixing his clear eyes significantly on Lagrange, "depends upon the chances of war, which you probably understand as well as I do."

"We should never think of making any calculation on the action of an officer of such infinite resources as General Brant," said Lagrange ironically.

"You will, no doubt, have an opportunity of stating your own case to the division commander," continued Brant, with an unmoved face. "And," he continued, turning for the first time to Captain Faulkner, "when you tell the commander what I believe to be the fact—from your name and resemblance—that you are a relation of the young lady who for the last three weeks has been an inmate of this house under a pass from Washington, you will, I have no doubt, favorably explain your own propinquity to my lines."

"My sister Tilly!" said the young officer impulsively. "But she is no longer here. She passed through the lines back to Washington yesterday. No," he added, with a light laugh, "I'm afraid that excuse won't count for to-day."

A sudden frown upon the face of the elder officer, added to the perfect ingenuousness of Faulkner's speech, satisfied Brant that he had not only elicited the truth, but that Miss Faulkner had been successful. But he was sincere in his suggestion that her relationship to the young officer would incline the division commander to look leniently upon his fault, for he was conscious of a singular satisfaction in thus being able to serve her. Of the real object of the two men before him he had no doubt. They were "the friends" of his wife, who were waiting for her outside the lines! Chance alone had saved her from being arrested with them, with the consequent exposure of her treachery before his own men, who, as yet, had no proof of her guilt, nor any suspicion of her actual identity. Meanwhile his own chance of conveying her with safety beyond his lines was not affected by the incident; the prisoners dare not reveal what they knew of her, and it was with a grim triumph that he thought of compassing her escape without their aid. Nothing of this, however, was visible in his face, which the younger man watched with a kind of boyish curiosity, while Colonel Lagrange regarded the ceiling with a politely repressed yawn. "I regret," concluded Brant, as he summoned the officer of the guard, "that I shall have to deprive you of each other's company during the time you are here; but I shall see that you, separately, want for nothing in your confinement."

"If this is with a view to separate interrogatory, general, I can retire now," said Lagrange, rising, with ironical politeness.

"I believe I have all the information I require," returned Brant, with undisturbed composure. Giving the necessary orders to his subaltern, he acknowledged with equal calm the formal salutes of the two prisoners as they were led away, and returned quickly to his bedroom above. He paused instinctively for a moment before the closed door, and listened. There was no sound from within. He unlocked the door, and opened it.

So quiet was the interior that for an instant, without glancing at the bed, he cast a quick look at the window, which, till then, he had forgotten, and which he remembered gave upon the veranda roof. But it was still closed, and as he approached the bed, he saw his wife still lying there, in the attitude in which he had left her. But her eyes were ringed, and slightly filmed, as if with recent tears.

It was perhaps this circumstance that softened his voice, still harsh with command, as he said,—

"I suppose you knew those two men?"

"Yes."

"And that I have put it out of their power to help you?"

"I do."

There was something so strangely submissive in her voice that he again looked suspiciously at her. But he was shocked to see that she was quite pale now, and that the fire had gone out of her dark eyes.

"Then I may tell you what is my plan to save you. But, first, you must find this mulatto woman who has acted as your double."

"She is here."

"Here?"

"Yes."

"How do you know it?" he asked, in quick suspicion.

"She was not to leave this place until she knew I was safe within our lines. I have some friends who are faithful to me." After a pause she added, "She has been here already."

He looked at her, startled. "Impossible—I"—

"You locked the door. Yes! but she has a second key. And even if she had not, there is another entrance from that closet. You do not know this house: you have been here two weeks; I spent two years of my life, as a girl, in this room."

An indescribable sensation came over him; he remembered how he had felt when he first occupied it; this was followed by a keen sense of shame on reflecting that he had been, ever since, but a helpless puppet in the power of his enemies, and that she could have escaped if she would, even now.

"Perhaps," he said grimly, "you have already arranged your plans?"

She looked at him with a singular reproachfulness even in her submission.

"I have only told her to be ready to change clothes with me and help me color my face and hands at the time appointed. I have left the rest to you."

"Then this is my plan. I have changed only a detail. You and she must both leave this house at the same time, by different exits, but one of them must be private—and unknown to my men. Do you know of such a one?"

"Yes," she said, "in the rear of the negro quarters."

"Good," he replied, "that will be your way out. She will leave here, publicly, through the parade, armed with a pass from me. She will be overhauled and challenged by the first sentry near the guardhouse, below the wall. She will be subjected to some delay and scrutiny, which she will, however, be able to pass better than you would. This will create the momentary diversion that we require. In the mean time, you will have left the house by the rear, and you will then keep in the shadow of the hedge until you can drop down along the Run, where it empties into the swamp. That," he continued, fixing his keen eyes upon her, "is the one weak point in the position of this place that is neither overlooked nor defended. But perhaps," he added again grimly, "you already know it."

"It is the marsh where the flowers grow, near the path where you met Miss Faulkner. I had crossed the marsh to give her a letter," she said slowly.

A bitter smile came over Brant's face, but passed as quickly.

"Enough," he said quietly, "I will meet you beside the Run, and cross the marsh with you until you are within hailing distance of your lines. I will be in plain clothes, Alice," he went on slowly, "for it will not be the commander of this force who accompanies you, but your husband, and, without disgracing his uniform, he will drop to your level; for the instant he passes his own lines, in disguise, he will become, like you, a spy, and amenable to its penalties."

Her eyes seemed suddenly to leap up to his with that strange look of awakening and enthusiasm which he had noted before. And in its complete prepossession of all her instincts she rose from the bed, unheeding her bared arms and shoulders and loosened hair, and stood upright before him. For an instant husband and wife regarded each other as unreservedly as in their own chamber at Robles.

"When shall I go?"

He glanced through the window already growing lighter with the coming dawn. The relief would pass in a few moments; the time seemed propitious.

"At once," he said. "I will send Rose to you."

But his wife had already passed into the closet, and was tapping upon some inner door. He heard the sound of hinges turning and the rustling of garments. She reappeared, holding the curtains of the closet together with her hand, and said,—

"Go! When she comes to your office for the pass, you will know that I have gone."

He turned away.

"Stop!" she said faintly.

He turned back. Her expression had again changed. Her face was deadly pale; a strange tremor seemed to have taken possession of her. Her hands dropped from the curtain. Her beautiful arms moved slightly forward; it seemed to him that she would in the next moment have extended them towards him. But even then she said hurriedly, "Go! Go!" and slipped again behind the curtains.

He quickly descended the stairs as the sound of trampling feet on the road, and the hurried word of command, announced the return of the scouting party. The officer had little report to make beyond the fact that a morning mist, creeping along the valley, prevented any further observation, and bade fair to interrupt their own communications with the camp. Everything was quiet in the west, although the enemy's lines along the ridge seemed to have receded.

Brant had listened impatiently, for a new idea had seized him. Hooker was of the party, and was the one man in whom he could partly confide, and obtain a disguise. He at once made his way to the commissary wagons—one of which he knew Hooker used as a tent. Hastily telling him that he wished to visit the pickets without recognition, he induced him to lend him his slouched hat and frock coat, leaving with him his own distinguishing tunic, hat, and sword. He resisted the belt and pistols which Hooker would have forced upon him. As he left the wagon he was amusedly conscious that his old companion was characteristically examining the garments he had left behind with mingled admiration and envy. But he did not know, as he slipped out of the camp, that Mr. Hooker was quietly trying them on, before a broken mirror in the wagon-head!

The gray light of that summer morning was already so strong that, to avoid detection, he quickly dropped into the shadow of the gully that sloped towards the Run. The hot mist which the scouts had seen was now lying like a tranquil sea between him and the pickets of the enemy's rear-guard, which it seemed to submerge, and was clinging in moist tenuous swathes—like drawn-out cotton wool—along the ridge, half obliterating its face. From the valley in the rear it was already stealing in a thin white line up the slope like the advance of a ghostly column, with a stealthiness that, in spite of himself, touched him with superstitious significance. A warm perfume, languid and treacherous—as from the swamp magnolia—seemed to rise from the half-hidden marsh. An ominous silence, that appeared to be a part of this veiling of all things under the clear opal-tinted sky above, was so little like the hush of rest and peace, that he half-yearned for the outburst of musketry and tumult of attack that might dispel it. All that he had ever heard or dreamed of the insidious South, with its languid subtleties of climate and of race, seemed to encompass him here.

But the next moment he saw the figure he was waiting for stealing towards him from the shadow of the gulley beneath the negro quarters.

Even in that uncertain light there was no mistaking the tall figure, the gaudily striped clinging gown and turbaned head. And then a strange revulsion of feeling, quite characteristic of the emotional side of his singular temperament, overcame him. He was taking leave of his wife—the dream of his youth—perhaps forever! It should be no parting in anger as at Robles; it should be with a tenderness that would blot out their past in their separate memories—God knows! it might even be that a parting at that moment was a joining of them in eternity. In his momentary exaltation it even struck him that it was a duty, no less sacred, no less unselfish than the one to which he had devoted his life. The light was growing stronger; he could hear voices in the nearest picket line, and the sound of a cough in the invading mist. He made a hurried sign to the on-coming figure to follow him, ran ahead, and halted at last in the cover of a hackmatack bush. Still gazing forward over the marsh, he stealthily held out his hand behind him as the rustling skirt came nearer. At last his hand was touched—but even at that touch he started and turned quickly.

It was not his wife, but Rose!—her mulatto double! Her face was rigid with fright, her beady eyes staring in their china sockets, her white teeth chattering. Yet she would have spoken.

"Hush!" he said, clutching her hand, in a fierce whisper. "Not a word!"

She was holding something white in her fingers; he snatched it quickly. It was a note from his wife—not in the disguised hand of her first warning, but in one that he remembered as if it were a voice from their past.

"Forgive me for disobeying you to save you from capture, disgrace, or death—which would have come to you where you were going! I have taken Rose's pass. You need not fear that your honor will suffer by it, for if I am stopped I shall confess that I took it from her. Think no more of me, Clarence, but only of yourself. You are in danger."

He crushed the letter in his hand.

"Tell me," he said in a fierce whisper, seizing her arm, "and speak low. When did you leave her?"

"Sho'ly just now!" gasped the frightened woman.

He flung her aside. There might be still time to overtake and save her before she reached the picket lines. He ran up the gully, and out on to the slope towards the first guard-post. But a familiar challenge reached his ear, and his heart stopped beating.

"Who goes there?"

There was a pause, a rattle of arms voices—another pause— and Brant stood breathlessly listening. Then the voice rose again slowly and clearly: "Pass the mulatto woman!"

Thank God! she was saved! But the thought had scarcely crossed his mind before it seemed to him that a blinding crackle of sparks burst out along the whole slope below the wall, a characteristic yell which he knew too well rang in his ears, and an undulating line of dusty figures came leaping like gray wolves out of the mist upon his pickets. He heard the shouts of his men falling back as they fired; the harsh commands of a few officers hurrying to their posts, and knew that he had been hopelessly surprised and surrounded!

He ran forward among his disorganized men. To his consternation no one seemed to heed him! Then the remembrance of his disguise flashed upon him. But he had only time to throw away his hat and snatch a sword from a falling lieutenant, before a scorching flash seemed to pass before his eyes and burn through his hair, and he dropped like a log beside his subaltern.

*****

An aching under the bandage around his head where a spent bullet had grazed his scalp, and the sound of impossible voices in his ears were all he knew as he struggled slowly back to consciousness again. Even then it still seemed a delusion,—for he was lying on a cot in his own hospital, yet with officers of the division staff around him, and the division commander himself standing by his side, and regarding him with an air of grave but not unkindly concern. But the wounded man felt instinctively that it was not the effect of his physical condition, and a sense of shame came suddenly over him, which was not dissipated by his superior's words. For, motioning the others aside, the major-general leaned over his cot, and said,—

"Until a few moments ago, the report was that you had been captured in the first rush of the rear-guard which we were rolling up for your attack, and when you were picked up, just now, in plain clothes on the slope, you were not recognized. The one thing seemed to be as improbable as the other," he added significantly.

The miserable truth flashed across Brant's mind. Hooker must have been captured in his clothes—perhaps in some extravagant sally—and had not been recognized in the confusion by his own officers. Nevertheless, he raised his eyes to his superior.

"You got my note?"

The general's brow darkened.

"Yes," he said slowly, "but finding you thus unprepared—I had been thinking just now that you had been deceived by that woman—or by others—and that it was a clumsy forgery." He stopped, and seeing the hopeless bewilderment in the face of the wounded man, added more kindly: "But we will not talk of that in your present condition. The doctor says a few hours will put you straight again. Get strong, for I want you to lose no time—for your own sake—to report yourself at Washington."

"Report myself—at Washington!" repeated Brant slowly.

"That was last night's order," said the commander, with military curtness. Then he burst out: "I don't understand it, Brant! I believe you have been misunderstood, misrepresented, perhaps maligned and I shall make it MY business to see the thing through—but those are the Department orders. And for the present—I am sorry to say you are relieved of your command."

He turned away, and Brant closed his eyes. With them it seemed to him that he closed his career. No one would ever understand his explanation—even had he been tempted to give one, and he knew he never would. Everything was over now! Even this wretched bullet had not struck him fairly, and culminated his fate as it might! For an instant, he recalled his wife's last offer to fly with him beyond the seas—beyond this cruel injustice—but even as he recalled it, he knew that flight meant the worst of all—a half-confession! But she had escaped! Thank God for that! Again and again in his hopeless perplexity this comfort returned to him,—he had saved her; he had done his duty. And harping upon this in his strange fatalism, it at last seemed to him that this was for what he had lived—for what he had suffered—for what he had fitly ended his career. Perhaps it was left for him now to pass his remaining years in forgotten exile—even as his father had—his father!—his breath came quickly at the thought—God knows! perhaps as wrongfully accused! It may have been a Providence that she had borne him no child, to whom this dreadful heritage could be again transmitted.

There was something of this strange and fateful resignation in his face, a few hours later, when he was able to be helped again into the saddle. But he could see in the eyes of the few comrades who commiseratingly took leave of him, a vague, half-repressed awe of some indefinite weakness in the man, that mingled with their heartfelt parting with a gallant soldier. Yet even this touched him no longer. He cast a glance at the house and the room where he had parted from her, at the slope from which she had passed—and rode away.

And then, as his figure disappeared down the road, the restrained commentary of wonder, surmise, and criticism broke out:—

"It must have been something mighty bad, for the old man, who swears by him, looked rather troubled. And it was deuced queer, you know, this changing clothes with somebody, just before this surprise!"

"Nonsense! It's something away back of that! Didn't you hear the old man say that the orders for him to report himself came from Washington LAST NIGHT? No!"—the speaker lowered his voice—"Strangeways says that he had regularly sold himself out to one of them d—d secesh woman spies! It's the old Marc Antony business over again!"

"Now I think of it," said a younger subaltern, "he did seem mightily taken with one of those quadroons or mulattoes he issued orders against. I suppose that was a blind for us! I remember the first day he saw her; he was regularly keen to know all about her."

Major Curtis gave a short laugh.

"That mulatto, Martin, was a white woman, burnt-corked! She was trying to get through the lines last night, and fell off a wall or got a knock on the head from a sentry's carbine. When she was brought in, Doctor Simmons set to washing the blood off her face; the cork came off and the whole thing came out. Brant hushed it up—and the woman, too—in his own quarters! It's supposed now that she got away somehow in the rush!"

"It goes further back than that, gentlemen," said the adjutant authoritatively. "They say his wife was a howling secessionist, four years ago, in California, was mixed up in a conspiracy, and he had to leave on account of it. Look how thick he and that Miss Faulkner became, before he helped HER off!"

"That's your jealousy, Tommy; she knew he was, by all odds, the biggest man here, and a good deal more, too, and you had no show!"

In the laugh that followed, it would seem that Brant's eulogy had been spoken and forgotten. But as Lieutenant Martin was turning away, a lingering corporal touched his cap.

"You were speaking of those prowling mulattoes, sir. You know the general passed one out this morning."

"So I have heard."

"I reckon she didn't get very far. It was just at the time that we were driven in by their first fire, and I think she got her share of it, too. Do you mind walking this way, sir!"

The lieutenant did not mind, although he rather languidly followed. When they had reached the top of the gully, the corporal pointed to what seemed to be a bit of striped calico hanging on a thorn bush in the ravine.

"That's her," said the corporal. "I know the dress; I was on guard when she was passed. The searchers, who were picking up our men, haven't got to her yet; but she ain't moved or stirred these two hours. Would you like to go down and see her?"

The lieutenant hesitated. He was young, and slightly fastidious as to unnecessary unpleasantness. He believed he would wait until the searchers brought her up, when the corporal might call him.

The mist came up gloriously from the swamp like a golden halo. And as Clarence Brant, already forgotten, rode moodily through it towards Washington, hugging to his heart the solitary comfort of his great sacrifice, his wife, Alice Brant, for whom he had made it, was lying in the ravine, dead and uncared for. Perhaps it was part of the inconsistency of her sex that she was pierced with the bullets of those she had loved, and was wearing the garments of the race that she had wronged.

PART III

CHAPTER I

It was sunset of a hot day at Washington. Even at that hour the broad avenues, which diverged from the Capitol like the rays of another sun, were fierce and glittering. The sterile distances between glowed more cruelly than ever, and pedestrians, keeping in the scant shade, hesitated on the curbstones before plunging into the Sahara-like waste of crossings. The city seemed deserted. Even that vast army of contractors, speculators, place-hunters, and lobbyists, which hung on the heels of the other army, and had turned this pacific camp of the nation into a battlefield of ignoble conflict and contention—more disastrous than the one to the South—had slunk into their holes in hotel back bedrooms, in shady barrooms, or in the negro quarters of Georgetown, as if the majestic, white-robed Goddess enthroned upon the dome of the Capitol had at last descended among them and was smiting to right and left with the flat and flash of her insufferable sword.

Into this stifling atmosphere of greed and corruption Clarence Brant stepped from the shadow of the War Department. For the last three weeks he had haunted its ante-rooms and audience-chambers, in the vain hope of righting himself before his superiors, who were content, without formulating charges against him, to keep him in this disgrace of inaction and the anxiety of suspense. Unable to ascertain the details of the accusation, and conscious of his own secret, he was debarred the last resort of demanding a court-martial, which he knew could only exonerate him by the exposure of the guilt of his wife, whom he still hoped had safely escaped. His division commander, in active operations in the field, had no time to help him at Washington. Elbowed aside by greedy contractors, forestalled by selfish politicians, and disdaining the ordinary method of influence, he had no friend to turn to. In his few years of campaigning he had lost his instinct of diplomacy, without acquiring a soldier's bluntness.

The nearly level rays of the sun forced him at last to turn aside into one of the openings of a large building—a famous caravansary of that hotel-haunted capital, and he presently found himself in the luxurious bar-room, fragrant with mint, and cool with ice-slabs piled symmetrically on its marble counters. A few groups of men were seeking coolness at small tables with glasses before them and palm-leaf fans in their hands, but a larger and noisier assemblage was collected before the bar, where a man, collarless and in his shirt-sleeves, with his back to the counter, was pretentiously addressing them. Brant, who had moodily dropped into a chair in the corner, after ordering a cooling drink as an excuse for his temporary refuge from the stifling street, half-regretted his enforced participation in their conviviality. But a sudden lowering of the speaker's voice into a note of gloomy significance seemed familiar to him. He glanced at him quickly, from the shadow of his corner. He was not mistaken—it was Jim Hooker!

For the first time in his life, Brant wished to evade him. In the days of his own prosperity his heart had always gone out towards this old companion of his boyhood; in his present humiliation his presence jarred upon him. He would have slipped away, but to do so he would have had to pass before the counter again, and Hooker, with the self-consciousness of a story-teller, had an eye on his audience. Brant, with a palm-leaf fan before his face, was obliged to listen.

"Yes, gentlemen," said Hooker, examining his glass dramatically, "when a man's been cooped up in a Rebel prison, with a death line before him that he's obliged to cross every time he wants a square drink, it seems sort of like a dream of his boyhood to be standin' here comf'ble before his liquor, alongside o' white men once more. And when he knows he's bin put to all that trouble jest to save the reputation of another man, and the secrets of a few high and mighty ones, it's almost enough to make his liquor go agin him." He stopped theatrically, seemed to choke emotionally over his brandy squash, but with a pause of dramatic determination finally dashed it down. "No, gentlemen," he continued gloomily, "I don't say what I'm back in Washington FOR—I don't say what I've been sayin' to myself when I've bin picking the weevils outer my biscuits in Libby Prison—but ef you don't see some pretty big men in the War Department obliged to climb down in the next few days, my name ain't Jim Hooker, of Hooker, Meacham & Co., Army Beef Contractors, and the man who saved the fight at Gray Oaks!"

The smile of satisfaction that went around his audience—an audience quick to seize the weakness of any performance—might have startled a vanity less oblivious than Hooker's; but it only aroused Brant's indignation and pity, and made his position still more intolerable. But Hooker, scornfully expectorating a thin stream of tobacco juice against the spittoon, remained for an instant gloomily silent.

"Tell us about the fight again," said a smiling auditor.

Hooker looked around the room with a certain dark suspiciousness, and then, in an affected lower voice, which his theatrical experience made perfectly audible, went on:—

"It ain't much to speak of, and if it wasn't for the principle of the thing, I wouldn't be talking. A man who's seen Injin fightin' don't go much on this here West Point fightin' by rule-of-three—but that ain't here or there! Well, I'd bin out a-scoutin'—just to help the boys along, and I was sittin' in my wagon about daybreak, when along comes a brigadier-general, and he looks into the wagon flap. I oughter to tell you first, gentlemen, that every minit he was expecting an attack—but he didn't let on a hint of it to me. 'How are you, Jim?' said he. 'How are you, general?' said I. 'Would you mind lendin' me your coat and hat?' says he. 'I've got a little game here with our pickets, and I don't want to be recognized.' 'Anything to oblige, general,' said I, and with that I strips off my coat and hat, and he peels and puts them on. 'Nearly the same figure, Jim,' he says, lookin' at me, 'suppose you try on my things and see.' With that he hands me his coat—full uniform, by G-d!—with the little gold cords and laces and the epaulettes with a star, and I puts it on—quite innocent-like. And then he says, handin' me his sword and belt, 'Same inches round the waist, I reckon,' and I puts that on too. 'You may as well keep 'em on till I come back,' says he, 'for it's mighty damp and malarious at this time around the swamp.' And with that he lights out. Well, gentlemen, I hadn't sat there five minutes before Bang! bang! rattle! rattle! kershiz! and I hears a yell. I steps out of the wagon; everything's quite dark, but the rattle goes on. Then along trots an orderly, leadin' a horse. 'Mount, general,' he says, 'we're attacked—the rear-guard's on us!'"

He paused, looked round his audience, and then in a lower voice, said darkly,—

"I ain't a fool, an' in that minute a man's brain works at high pressure, and I saw it all! I saw the little game of the brigadier to skunk away in my clothes and leave me to be captured in his. But I ain't a dog neither, and I mounted that horse, gentlemen, and lit out to where the men were formin'! I didn't dare to speak, lest they should know me, but I waved my sword, and by G-d! they followed me! And the next minit we was in the thick of it. I had my hat as full of holes as that ice strainer; I had a dozen bullets through my coat, the fringe of my epaulettes was shot away, but I kept the boys at their work—and we stopped 'em! Stopped 'em, gentlemen, until we heard the bugles of the rest of our division, that all this time had been rolling that blasted rear-guard over on us! And it saved the fight; but the next minute the Johnny Rebs made a last dash and cut me off—and there I was—by G-d, a prisoner! Me that had saved the fight!"

A ripple of ironical applause went round as Hooker gloomily drained his glass, and then held up his hand in scornful deprecation.

"I said I was a prisoner, gentlemen," he went on bitterly; "but that ain't all! I asked to see Johnston, told him what I had done, and demanded to be exchanged for a general officer. He said, 'You be d—d.' I then sent word to the division commander-in-chief, and told him how I had saved Gray Oaks when his brigadier ran away, and he said, 'You be d— d.' I've bin 'You be d—d' from the lowest non-com. to the commander-in-chief, and when I was at last exchanged, I was exchanged, gentlemen, for two mules and a broken wagon. But I'm here, gentlemen—as I was thar!"

"Why don't you see the President about it?" asked a bystander, in affected commiseration.

Mr. Hooker stared contemptuously at the suggestion, and

expectorated his scornful dissent.

"Not much!" he said. "But I'm going to see the man that carries him and his Cabinet in his breeches-pocket—Senator Boompointer."

"Boompointer's a big man," continued his auditor doubtfully. "Do you know him?"

"Know him?" Mr. Hooker laughed a bitter, sardonic laugh. "Well, gentlemen, I ain't the kind o' man to go in for family influence; but," he added, with gloomy elevation, "considering he's an intimate relation of mine, BY MARRIAGE, I should say I did."

Brant heard no more; the facing around of his old companion towards the bar gave him that opportunity of escaping he had been waiting for. The defection of Hooker and his peculiar inventions were too characteristic of him to excite surprise, and, although they no longer awakened his good-humored tolerance, they were powerless to affect him in his greater trouble. Only one thing he learned—that Hooker knew nothing of his wife being in camp as a spy—the incident would have been too tempting to have escaped his dramatic embellishment. And the allusion to Senator Boompointer, monstrous as it seemed in Hooker's mouth, gave him a grim temptation. He had heard of Boompointer's wonderful power; he believed that Susy would and could help him— Clarence—whether she did or did not help Hooker. But the next moment he dismissed the idea, with a flushing cheek. How low had he already sunk, even to think of it!

It had been once or twice in his mind to seek the President, and, under a promise of secrecy, reveal a part of his story. He had heard many anecdotes of his goodness of heart and generous tolerance of all things, but with this was joined—so said contemporaneous history—a flippancy of speech and a brutality of directness from which Clarence's sensibility shrank. Would he see anything in his wife but a common spy on his army; would he see anything in him but the weak victim, like many others, of a scheming woman? Stories current in camp and Congress of the way that this grim humorist had, with an apposite anecdote or a rugged illustration, brushed away the most delicate sentiment or the subtlest poetry, even as he had exposed the sham of Puritanic morality or of Epicurean ethics. Brant had even solicited an audience, but had retired awkwardly, and with his confidence unspoken, before the dark, humorous eyes, that seemed almost too tolerant of his grievance. He had been to levees, and his heart had sunk equally before the vulgar crowd, who seemed to regard this man as their own buffoon, and the pompousness of position, learning and dignity, which he seemed to delight to shake and disturb.

One afternoon, a few days later, in sheer listlessness of purpose, he found himself again at the White House. The President was giving audience to a deputation of fanatics, who, with a pathetic simplicity almost equal to his own pathetic tolerance, were urging upon this ruler of millions the policy of an insignificant score, and Brant listened to his patient, practical response of facts and logic, clothed in simple but sinewy English, up to the inevitable climax of humorous illustration, which the young brigadier could now see was necessary to relieve the grimness of his refusal. For the first time Brant felt the courage to address him, and resolved to wait until the deputation retired. As they left the gallery he lingered in the ante-room for the President to appear. But, as he did not come, afraid of losing his chances, he returned to the gallery. Alone in his privacy and shadow, the man he had just left was standing by a column, in motionless abstraction, looking over the distant garden. But the kindly, humorous face was almost tragic with an intensity of weariness! Every line of those strong, rustic features was relaxed under a burden which even the long, lank, angular figure—overgrown and unfinished as his own West—seemed to be distorted in its efforts to adjust itself to; while the dark, deep-set eyes were abstracted with the vague prescience of the prophet and the martyr. Shocked at that sudden change, Brant felt his cheek burn with shame. And he was about to break upon that wearied man's unbending; he was about to add his petty burden to the shoulders of this Western Atlas. He drew back silently, and descended the stairs.

But before he had left the house, while mingling with the crowd in one of the larger rooms, he saw the President reappear beside an important, prosperous-looking figure, on whom the kindly giant was now smiling with humorous toleration. He noticed the divided attention of the crowd; the name of Senator Boompointer was upon every lip; he was nearly face to face with that famous dispenser of place and preferment—this second husband of Susy! An indescribable feeling—half cynical, half fateful—came over him. He would not have been surprised to see Jim Hooker join the throng, which now seemed to him to even dwarf the lonely central figure that had so lately touched him! He wanted to escape it all!

But his fate brought him to the entrance at the same moment that Boompointer was leaving it, and that distinguished man brushed hastily by him as a gorgeous carriage, drawn by two spirited horses, and driven by a resplendent negro coachman, dashed up. It was the Boompointer carriage.

A fashionably-dressed, pretty woman, who, in style, bearing, opulent contentment, and ingenuous self-consciousness, was in perfect keeping with the slight ostentation of the equipage, was its only occupant. As Boompointer stepped into the vehicle, her blue eyes fell for an instant on Brant. A happy, childlike pink flush came into her cheeks, and a violet ray of recognition and mischief darted from her eyes to his. For it was Susy.

CHAPTER II

When Brant returned to his hotel there was an augmented respect in the voice of the clerk as he handed him a note with the remark that it had been left by Senator Boompointer's coachman. He had no difficulty in recognizing Susy's peculiarly Brobdingnagian school-girl hand.

"Kla'uns, I call it real mean! I believe you just HOPED I wouldn't know you. If you're a bit like your old self you'll come right off here—this very night! I've got a big party on—but we can talk somewhere between the acts! Haven't I growed? Tell me! And my! what a gloomy swell the young brigadier is! The carriage will come for you—so you have no excuse."

The effect of this childish note upon Brant was strangely out of proportion to its triviality. But then it was Susy's very triviality—so expressive of her characteristic irrespon-sibility—which had always affected him at such moments. Again, as at Robles, he felt it react against his own ethics. Was she not right in her delightful materialism? Was she not happier than if she had been consistently true to Mrs. Peyton, to the convent, to the episode of her theatrical career, to Jim Hooker—even to himself? And did he conscientiously believe that Hooker or himself had suffered from her inconsistency? No! From all that he had heard, she was a suitable helpmate to the senator, in her social attractiveness, her charming ostentations, her engaging vanity that disarmed suspicion, and her lack of responsibility even in her partisanship. Nobody ever dared to hold the senator responsible for her promises, even while enjoying the fellowship of both, and it is said that the worthy man singularly profited by it. Looking upon the invitation as a possible distraction to his gloomy thoughts, Brant resolved to go.

The moon was high as the carriage whirled him out of the still stifling avenues towards the Soldiers' Home—a sylvan suburb frequented by cabinet ministers and the President—where the good Senator had "decreed," like Kubla Khan, "a stately pleasure dome," to entertain his friends and partisans. As they approached the house, the trembling light like fireflies through the leaves, the warm silence broken only by a military band playing a drowsy waltz on the veranda, and the heavy odors of jessamine in the air, thrilled Brant with a sense of shame as he thought of his old comrades in the field. But this was presently dissipated by the uniforms that met him in the hall, with the presence of some of his distinguished superiors. At the head of the stairs, with a circling background of the shining crosses and ribbons of the diplomatic corps, stood Susy—her bare arms and neck glittering with diamonds, her face radiant with childlike vivacity. A significant pressure of her little glove as he made his bow seemed to be his only welcome, but a moment later she caught his arm. "You've yet to know HIM," she said in a half whisper; "he thinks a good deal of himself—just like Jim. But he makes others believe it, and that's where poor Jim slipped up." She paused before the man thus characteristically disposed of, and presented Brant. It was the man he had seen before—material, capable, dogmatic. A glance from his shrewd eyes—accustomed to the weighing of men's weaknesses and ambitions—and a few hurried phrases, apparently satisfied him that Brant was not just then important or available to him, and the two men, a moment later, drifted easily apart. Brant sauntered listlessly through the crowded rooms, half remorsefully conscious that he had taken some irrevocable step, and none the less assured by the presence of two or three reporters and correspondents who were dogging his steps, or the glance of two or three pretty women whose curiosity had evidently been aroused by the singular abstraction of this handsome, distinguished, but sardonic-looking officer. But the next moment he was genuinely moved.

A tall young woman had just glided into the centre of the room with an indolent yet supple gracefulness that seemed familiar to him. A change in her position suddenly revealed her face. It was Miss Faulkner. Previously he had known her only in the riding habit of Confederate gray which she had at first affected, or in the light muslin morning dress she had worn at Gray Oaks. It seemed to him, to-night, that the studied elegance of her full dress became her still more; that the pretty willfulness of her chin and shoulders was chastened and modified by the pearls round her fair throat. Suddenly their eyes met; her face paled visibly; he fancied that she almost leaned against her companion for support; then she met his glance again with a face into which the color had as suddenly rushed, but with eyes that seemed to be appealing to him even to the point of pain and fright. Brant was not conceited; he could see that the girl's agitation was not the effect of any mere personal influence in his recognition, but of something else. He turned hastily away; when he looked around again she was gone.

Nevertheless he felt filled with a vague irritation. Did she think him such a fool as to imperil her safety by openly recognizing her without her consent? Did she think that he would dare to presume upon the service she had done him? Or, more outrageous thought, had she heard of his disgrace, known its cause, and feared that he would drag her into a disclosure to save himself? No, no; she could not think that! She had perhaps regretted what she had done in a freak of girlish chivalry; she had returned to her old feelings and partisanship; she was only startled at meeting the single witness of her folly. Well, she need not fear! He would as studiously avoid her hereafter, and she should know it. And yet—yes, there was a "yet." For he could not forget—indeed, in the past three weeks it had been more often before him than he cared to think—that she was the one human being who had been capable of a great act of self-sacrifice for him—her enemy, her accuser, the man who had scarcely treated her civilly. He was ashamed to remember now that this thought had occurred to him at the bedside of his wife—at the hour of her escape—even on the fatal slope on which he had been struck down. And now this fond illusion must go with the rest—the girl who had served him so loyally was ashamed of it! A bitter smile crossed his face.

"Well, I don't wonder! Here are all the women asking me who is that good-looking Mephistopheles, with the burning eyes, who is prowling around my rooms as if searching for a victim. Why, you're smiling for all the world like poor Jim when he used to do the Red Avenger."

Susy's voice—and illustration—recalled him to himself.

"Furious I may be," he said with a gentler smile, although his eyes still glittered, "furious that I have to wait until the one woman I came to see—the one woman I have not seen for so long, while these puppets have been nightly dancing before her—can give me a few moments from them, to talk of the old days."

In his reaction he was quite sincere, although he felt a slight sense of remorse as he saw the quick, faint color rise, as in those old days, even through the to-night's powder of her cheek.

"That's like the old Kla'uns," she said, with a slight pressure of his arm, "but we will not have a chance to speak until later. When they are nearly all gone, you'll take me to get a little refreshment, and we'll have a chat in the conservatory. But you must drop that awfully wicked look and make yourself generally agreeable to those women until then."

It was, perhaps, part of this reaction which enabled him to obey his hostess' commands with a certain recklessness that, however, seemed to be in keeping with the previous Satanic reputation he had all unconsciously achieved. The women listened to the cynical flippancy of this good-looking soldier with an undisguised admiration which in turn excited curiosity and envy from his own sex. He saw the whispered questioning, the lifted eyebrows, scornful shrugging of shoulders—and knew that the story of his disgrace was in the air. But I fear this only excited him to further recklessness and triumph. Once he thought he recognized Miss Faulkner's figure at a distance, and even fancied that she had been watching him; but he only redoubled his attentions to the fair woman beside him, and looked no more.

Yet he was glad when the guests began to drop off, the great rooms thinned, and Susy, appearing on the arm of her husband, coquettishly reminded him of his promise.

"For I want to talk to you of old times. General Brant," she went on, turning explanatorily to Boompointer, "married my adopted mother in California—at Robles, a dear old place where I spent my earliest years. So, you see, we are sort of relations by marriage," she added, with delightful naivete.

Hooker's own vainglorious allusion to his relations to the

man before him flashed across Brant's mind, but it left now only a smile on his lips. He felt he had already become a part of the irresponsible comedy played around him. Why should he resist, or examine its ethics too closely? He offered his arm to Susy as they descended the stairs, but, instead of pausing in the supper-room, she simply passed through it with a significant pressure on his arm, and, drawing aside a muslin curtain, stepped into the moonlit conservatory. Behind the curtain there was a small rustic settee; without releasing his arm she sat down, so that when he dropped beside her, their hands met, and mutually clasped.

"Now, Kla'uns," she said, with a slight, comfortable shiver as she nestled beside him, "it's a little like your chair down at old Robles, isn't it?—tell me! And to think it's five years ago! But, Kla'uns, what's the matter? You are changed," she said, looking at his dark face in the moonlight, "or you have something to tell me."

"I have."

"And it's something dreadful, I know!" she said, wrinkling her brows with a pretty terror. "Couldn't you pretend you had told it to me, and let us go on just the same? Couldn't you, Kla'uns? Tell me!"

"I am afraid I couldn't," he said, with a sad smile.

"Is it about yourself, Kla'uns? You know," she went on with cheerful rapidity, "I know everything about you—I always did, you know—and I don't care, and never did care, and it don't, and never did, make the slightest difference to me. So don't tell it, and waste time, Kla'uns."

"It's not about me, but about my wife!" he said slowly.

Her expression changed slightly

"Oh, her!" she said after a pause. Then, half-resignedly, "Go on, Kla'uns."

He began. He had a dozen times rehearsed to himself his miserable story, always feeling it keenly, and even fearing that he might be carried away by emotion or morbid sentiment in telling it to another. But, to his astonishment, he found himself telling it practically, calmly, almost cynically, to his old playmate, repressing the half devotion and even tenderness that had governed him, from the time that his wife, disguised as the mulatto woman, had secretly watched him at his office, to the hour that he had passed through the lines. He withheld only the incident of Miss Faulkner's complicity and sacrifice.

"And she got away, after having kicked you out of your place, Kla'uns?" said Susy, when he had ended.

Clarence stiffened beside her. But he felt he had gone too far to quarrel with his confidante.

"She went away. I honestly believe we shall never meet again, or I should not be telling you this!"

"Kla'uns," she said lightly, taking his hand again, "don't you believe it! She won't let you go. You're one of those men that a woman, when she's once hooked on to, won't let go of, even when she believes she no longer loves him, or meets bigger and better men. I reckon it's because you're so different from other men; maybe there are so many different things about you to hook on to, and you don't slip off as easily as the others. Now, if you were like old Peyton, her first husband, or like poor Jim, or even my Boompointer, you'd be all right! No, my boy, all we can do is to try to keep her from getting at you here. I reckon she won't trust herself in Washington again in a hurry."

"But I cannot stay here; my career is in the field."

"Your career is alongside o' me, honey—and Boompointer. But nearer ME. We'll fix all that. I heard something about your being in disgrace, but the story was that you were sweet on some secesh girl down there, and neglected your business, Kla'uns. But, Lordy! to think it was only your own wife! Never mind; we'll straighten that out. We've had worse jobs than that on. Why, there was that commissary who was buying up dead horses at one end of the field, and selling them to the Government for mess beef at the other; and there was that general who wouldn't make an attack when it rained; and the other general—you know who I mean, Kla'uns—who wouldn't invade the State where his sister lived; but we straightened them out, somehow, and they were a heap worse than you. We'll get you a position in the war department here, one of the bureau offices, where you keep your rank and your uniform—you don't look bad in it, Kla'uns—on better pay. And you'll come and see me, and we'll talk over old times."

Brant felt his heart turn sick within him. But he was at her mercy now! He said, with an effort,—

"But I've told you that my career—nay, my LIFE—now is in the field."

"Don't you be a fool, Kla'uns, and leave it there! You have done your work of fighting—mighty good fighting, too,— and everybody knows it. You've earned a change. Let others take your place."

He shuddered, as he remembered that his wife had made the

same appeal. Was he a fool then, and these two women—so totally unlike in everything—right in this?

"Come, Kla'uns," said Susy, relapsing again against his shoulder. "Now talk to me! You don't say what you think of me, of my home, of my furniture, of my position—even of him! Tell me!"

"I find you well, prosperous, and happy," he said, with a faint smile.

"Is that all? And how do I look?"

She turned her still youthful, mischievous face towards him in the moonlight. The witchery of her blue eyes was still there as of old, the same frank irresponsibility beamed from them; her parted lips seemed to give him back the breath of his youth. He started, but she did not.

"Susy, dear!"

It was her husband's voice.

"I quite forgot," the Senator went on, as he drew the curtain aside, "that you are engaged with a friend; but Miss Faulkner is waiting to say good-night, and I volunteered to find you."

"Tell her to wait a moment," said Susy, with an impatience that was as undisguised as it was without embarrassment or confusion.

But Miss Faulkner, unconsciously following Mr. Boompointer, was already upon them. For a moment the whole four were silent, although perfectly composed. Senator Boompointer, unconscious of any infelicity in his interruption, was calmly waiting. Clarence, opposed suddenly to the young girl whom he believed was avoiding his recognition, rose, coldly imperturbable. Miss Faulkner, looking taller and more erect in the long folds of her satin cloak, neither paled nor blushed, as she regarded Susy and Brant with a smile of well-bred apology.

"I expect to leave Washington to-morrow, and may not be able to call again," she said, "or I would not have so particularly pressed a leave-taking upon you."

"I was talking with my old friend, General Brant," said Susy, more by way of introduction than apology.

Brant bowed. For an instant the clear eyes of Miss Faulkner slipped icily across his as she made him an old-fashioned Southern courtesy, and, taking Susy's arm, she left the room. Brant did not linger, but took leave of his host almost in the same breath. At the front door a well-appointed carriage of one of the Legations had just rolled into waiting. He looked back; he saw Miss Faulkner, erect and looking like a bride in her gauzy draperies, descending the stairs before the waiting servants. He felt his heart beat strangely. He hesitated, recalled himself with an effort, hurriedly stepped from the porch into the path, as he heard the carriage door close behind him in the distance, and then felt the dust from her horse's hoofs rise around him as she drove past him and away.

CHAPTER III

Although Brant was convinced as soon as he left the house that he could not accept anything from the Boompointer influence, and that his interview with Susy was fruitless, he knew that he must temporize. While he did not believe that his old playmate would willingly betray him, he was uneasy when he thought of the vanity and impulsiveness which might compromise him—or of a possible jealousy that might seek revenge. Yet he had no reason to believe that Susy's nature was jealous, or that she was likely to have any cause; but the fact remained that Miss Faulkner's innocent intrusion upon their tete-a-tete affected him more strongly than anything else in his interview with Susy. Once out of the atmosphere of that house, it struck him, too, that Miss Faulkner was almost as much of an alien in it as himself. He wondered what she had been doing there. Could it be possible that she was obtaining information for the South? But he rejected the idea as quickly as it had occurred to him. Perhaps there could be no stronger proof of the unconscious influence the young girl already had over him.

He remembered the liveries of the diplomatic carriage that had borne her away, and ascertained without difficulty that her sister had married one of the foreign ministers, and that she was a guest in his house. But he was the more astonished to hear that she and her sister were considered to be Southern

Unionists—and were greatly petted in governmental circles for their sacrificing fidelity to the flag. His informant, an official in the State Department, added that Miss Matilda might have been a good deal of a madcap at the outbreak of the war—for the sisters had a brother in the Confederate service—but that she had changed greatly, and, indeed, within a month. "For," he added, "she was at the White House for the first time last week, and they say the President talked more to her than to any other woman."

The indescribable sensation with which this simple information filled Brant startled him more than the news itself. Hope, joy, fear, distrust, and despair, alternately distracted him. He recalled Miss Faulkner's almost agonizing glance of appeal to him in the drawing-room at Susy's, and it seemed to be equally consistent with the truth of what he had just heard—or some monstrous treachery and deceit of which she might be capable. Even now she might be a secret emissary of some spy within the President's family; she might have been in correspondence with some traitor in the Boompointer clique, and her imploring glance only the result of a fear of exposure. Or, again, she might have truly recanted after her escapade at Gray Oaks, and feared only his recollection of her as go-between of spies. And yet both of these presumptions were inconsistent with her conduct in the conservatory. It seemed impossible that this impulsive woman, capable of doing what he had himself known her to do, and equally sensitive to the shame or joy of such impulses, should be the same conventional woman of society who had so coldly recognized and parted from him.

But this interval of doubt was transitory. The next day he received a dispatch from the War Department, ordering him to report himself for duty at once. With a beating heart he hurried to the Secretary. But that official had merely left a memorandum with his assistant directing General Brant to accompany some fresh levies to a camp of "organization" near the front. Brant felt a chill of disappointment. Duties of this kind had been left to dubious regular army veterans, hurriedly displaced general officers, and favored detrimentals. But if it was not restoration, it was no longer inaction, and it was at least a release from Washington.

It was also evidently the result of some influence—but hardly that of the Boompointers, for he knew that Susy wished to keep him at the Capital. Was there another power at work to send him away from Washington? His previous doubts returned. Nor were they dissipated when the chief of the bureau placed a letter before him with the remark that it had been entrusted to him by a lady with the request that it should be delivered only into his own hands.

"She did not know your hotel address, but ascertained you were to call here. She said it was of some importance. There is no mystery about it, General," continued the official with a mischievous glance at Brant's handsome, perplexed face, "although it's from a very pretty woman—whom we all know."

"Mrs. Boompointer?" suggested Brant, with affected lightness.

It was a maladroit speech. The official's face darkened.

"We have not yet become a Postal Department for the Boompointers, General," he said dryly, "however great their influence elsewhere. It was from rather a different style of woman—Miss Faulkner. You will receive your papers later at your hotel, and leave to-night."

Brant's unlucky slip was still potent enough to divert the official attention, or he would have noticed the change in his visitor's face, and the abruptness of his departure.

Once in the street, Brant tore off the envelope. But beneath it was another, on which was written in a delicate, refined hand: "Please do not open this until you reach your destination."

Then she knew he was going! And perhaps this was her influence? All his suspicions again returned. She knew he was going near the lines, and his very appointment, through her power, might be a plot to serve her and the enemy! Was this letter, which she was entrusting to him, the cover of some missive to her Southern friends which she expected him to carry—perhaps as a return for her own act of self-sacrifice? Was this the appeal she had been making to his chivalry, his gratitude, his honor? The perspiration stood in beads on his forehead. What defect lay hidden in his nature that seemed to make him an easy victim of these intriguing women? He had not even the excuse of gallantry; less susceptible to the potencies of the sex than most men, he was still compelled to bear that reputation. He remembered his coldness to Miss Faulkner in the first days of their meeting, and her effect upon his subalterns. Why had she selected him from among them—when she could have modeled the others like wax to her purposes? Why? And yet with the question came a possible answer that he hardly dared to think of—that in its very vagueness seemed to fill him with a stimulating thrill and hopefulness. He quickened his pace. He would take the letter, and yet be master of himself when the time came to open it.

That time came three days later, in his tent at Three Pines Crossing. As he broke open the envelope, he was relieved to find that it contained no other inclosure, and seemed intended only for himself. It began abruptly:—

"When you read this, you will understand why I did not speak to you when we met last night; why I even dreaded that you might speak to me, knowing, as I did, what I ought to tell you at that place and moment—something you could only know from me. I did not know you were in Washington, although I knew you were relieved; I had no way of seeing you or sending to you before, and I only came to Mrs. Boompointer's party in the hope of hearing news of you.

"You know that my brother was captured by your pickets in company with another officer. He thinks you suspected the truth—that he and his friend were hovering near your lines to effect the escape of the spy. But he says that, although they failed to help her, she did escape, or was passed through the lines by your connivance. He says that you seemed to know her, that from what Rose—the mulatto woman—told him, you and she were evidently old friends. I would not speak of this, nor intrude upon your private affairs, only that I think you ought to know that I had no knowledge of it when I was in your house, but believed her to be a stranger to you. You gave me no intimation that you knew her, and I believed that you were frank with me. But I should not speak of this at all—for I believe that it would have made no difference to me in repairing the wrong that I thought I had done you— only that, as I am forced by circumstances to tell you the terrible ending of this story, you ought to know it all.

"My brother wrote to me that the evening after you left, the burying party picked up the body of what they believed to be a mulatto woman lying on the slope. It was not Rose, but the body of the very woman—the real and only spy—whom you had passed through the lines. She was accidentally killed by the Confederates in the first attack upon you, at daybreak. But only my brother and his friend recognized her through her blackened face and disguise, and on the plea that she was a servant of one of their friends, they got permission from the division commander to take her away, and she was buried by her friends and among her people in the little cemetery of Three Pines Crossing, not far from where you have gone. My brother thought that I ought to tell you this: it seems that he and his friend had a strange sympathy for you in what they appear to know or guess of your relations with that woman, and I think he was touched by what he thought was your kindness and chivalry to him on account of his sister. But I do not think he ever knew, or will know, how great is the task that he has imposed upon me.

"You know now, do you not, WHY I did not speak to you when we first met; it seemed so impossible to do it in an atmosphere and a festivity that was so incongruous with the dreadful message I was charged with. And when I had to meet you later—perhaps I may have wronged you—but it seemed to me that you were so preoccupied and interested with other things that I might perhaps only be wearying you with something you cared little for, or perhaps already knew and had quickly forgotten.

"I had been wanting to say something else to you when I had got rid of my dreadful message. I do not know if you still care to hear it. But you were once generous enough to think that I had done you a service in bringing a letter to your commander. Although I know better than anybody else the genuine devotion to your duty that made you accept my poor service, from all that I can hear, you have never had the credit of it. Will you not try me again? I am more in favor here, and I might yet be more successful in showing your superiors how true you have been to your trust, even if you have little faith in your friend, Matilda Faulkner."

For a long time he remained motionless, with the letter in his hand. Then he arose, ordered his horse, and galloped away.

There was little difficulty in finding the cemetery of Three Pines Crossing—a hillside slope, hearsed with pine and cypress, and starred with white crosses, that in the distance looked like flowers. Still less was there in finding the newer marble shaft among the older lichen-spotted slabs, which bore the simple words: "Alice Benham, Martyr." A few Confederate soldiers, under still plainer and newer wooden headstones, carved only with initials, lay at her feet. Brant sank on his knees beside the grave, but he was shocked to see that the base of the marble was stained with the red pollen of the fateful lily, whose blossoms had been heaped upon her mound, but whose fallen petals lay dark and sodden in decay.

How long he remained there he did not know. And then a solitary bugle from the camp seemed to summon him, as it had once before summoned him, and he went away—as he had gone before—to a separation that he now knew was for all time.

Then followed a month of superintendence and drill, and the infusing into the little camp under his instruction the spirit which seemed to be passing out of his own life forever. Shut in by alien hills on the borderland of the great struggle, from time to time reports reached him of the bitter fighting, and almost disastrous successes of his old division commander. Orders came from Washington to hurry the preparation of his raw levies to the field, and a faint hope sprang up in his mind. But following it came another dispatch ordering his return to the Capital.

He reached it with neither hope nor fear—so benumbed had become his spirit under this last trial, and what seemed to be now the mockery of this last sacrifice to his wife. Though it was no longer a question of her life and safety, he knew that he could still preserve her memory from stain by keeping her secret, even though its divulgings might clear his own. For that reason, he had even hesitated to inform Susy of her

Bret Harte

death, in the fear that, in her thoughtless irresponsibility and impulsiveness, she might be tempted to use it in his favor. He had made his late appointment a plea for her withholding any present efforts to assist him. He even avoided the Boompointers' house, in what he believed was partly a duty to the memory of his wife. But he saw no inconsistency in occasionally extending his lonely walks to the vicinity of a foreign Legation, or in being lifted with a certain expectation at the sight of its liveries on the Avenue. There was a craving for sympathy in his heart, which Miss Faulkner's letter had awakened.

Meantime, he had reported himself for duty at the War Department—with little hope, however, in that formality. But he was surprised the next day when the chief of the bureau informed him that his claim was before the President.

"I was not aware that I had presented any claim," he said, a little haughtily.

The bureau chief looked up with some surprise. This quiet, patient, reserved man had puzzled him once or twice before.

"Perhaps I should say 'case,' General," he said, drily. "But the personal interest of the highest executive in the land strikes me as being desirable in anything."

"I only mean that I have obeyed the orders of the department in reporting myself here, as I have done," said Brant, with less feeling, but none the less firmness; "and I should imagine it was not the duty of a soldier to question them. Which I fancy a 'claim' or a 'case' would imply."

He had no idea of taking this attitude before, but the disappointments of the past month, added to this first official notice of his disgrace, had brought forward that dogged, reckless, yet half-scornful obstinacy that was part of his nature.

The official smiled.

"I suppose, then, you are waiting to hear from the President," he said drily.

"I am awaiting orders from the department," returned Brant quietly, "but whether they originate in the President as commander-in-chief, or not—it is not for me to inquire."

Even when he reached his hotel this half-savage indifference which had taken the place of his former incertitude had not changed. It seemed to him that he had reached the crisis of his life where he was no longer a free agent, and could wait, superior alike to effort or expectation. And it was with a merely dispassionate curiosity that he found a note the next morning from the President's private secretary, informing him that the President would see him early that day.

A few hours later he was ushered through the public rooms of the White House to a more secluded part of the household. The messenger stopped before a modest door and knocked. It was opened by a tall figure—the President himself. He reached out a long arm to Brant, who stood hesitatingly on the threshold, grasped his hand, and led him into the room. It had a single, large, elaborately draped window and a handsome medallioned carpet, which contrasted with the otherwise almost appalling simplicity of the furniture. A single plain angular desk, with a blotting pad and a few sheets of large foolscap upon it, a waste-paper basket and four plain armchairs, completed the interior with a contrast as simple and homely as its long-limbed, black-coated occupant. Releasing the hand of the general to shut a door which opened into another apartment, the President shoved an armchair towards him and sank somewhat wearily into another before the desk. But only for a moment; the long shambling limbs did not seem to adjust themselves easily to the chair; the high narrow shoulders drooped to find a more comfortable lounging attitude, shifted from side to side, and the long legs moved dispersedly. Yet the face that was turned towards Brant was humorous and tranquil.

"I was told I should have to send for you if I wished to see you," he said smilingly.

Already mollified, and perhaps again falling under the previous influence of this singular man, Brant began somewhat hesitatingly to explain.

But the President checked him gently,—

"You don't understand. It was something new to my experience here to find an able-bodied American citizen with an honest genuine grievance who had to have it drawn from him like a decayed tooth. But you have been here before. I seem to remember your face."

Brant's reserve had gone. He admitted that he had twice sought an audience—but—

"You dodged the dentist! That was wrong." As Brant made a slight movement of deprecation the President continued: "I understand! Not from fear of giving pain to yourself but to others. I don't know that THAT is right, either. A certain amount of pain must be suffered in this world—even by one's enemies. Well, I have looked into your case, General Brant." He took up a piece of paper from his desk, scrawled with two or three notes in pencil. "I think this is the way it stands. You were commanding a position at Gray Oaks when information was received by the department that, either through neglect or complicity, spies were passing through your lines. There was no attempt to prove your neglect; your orders, the facts of your personal care and precaution, were all before the department. But it was also shown that your wife, from whom you were only temporarily separated, was a notorious secessionist; that, before the war, you yourself were suspected, and that, therefore, you were quite capable of evading your own orders, which you may have only given as a blind. On this information you were relieved by the department of your command. Later on it was discovered that the spy was none other than your own wife, disguised as a mulatto; that, after her arrest by your own soldiers, you connived at her escape—and this was considered conclusive proof of—well, let us say—your treachery."

"But I did not know it was my wife until she was arrested," said Brant impulsively.

The President knitted his eyebrows humorously.

"Don't let us travel out of the record, General. You're as bad as the department. The question was one of your personal treachery, but you need not accept the fact that you were justly removed because your wife was a spy. Now, General, I am an old lawyer, and I don't mind telling you that in Illinois we wouldn't hang a yellow dog on that evidence before the department. But when I was asked to look into the matter by your friends, I discovered something of more importance to you. I had been trying to find a scrap of evidence that would justify the presumption that you had sent information to the enemy. I found that it was based upon the fact of the enemy being in possession of knowledge at the first battle at Gray Oaks, which could only have been obtained from our side, and which led to a Federal disaster; that you, however, retrieved by your gallantry. I then asked the secretary if he was prepared to show that you had sent the information with that view, or that you had been overtaken by a tardy sense of repentance. He preferred to consider my suggestion as humorous. But the inquiry led to my further discovery that the only treasonable correspondence actually in evidence was found upon the body of a trusted Federal officer, and had been forwarded to the division commander. But there was no record of it in the case."

"Why, I forwarded it myself," said Brant eagerly.

"So the division commander writes," said the President, smiling, "and he forwarded it to the department. But it was suppressed in some way. Have you any enemies, General Brant?"

"Not that I know of."

"Then you probably have. You are young and successful. Think of the hundred other officers who naturally believe themselves better than you are, and haven't a traitorous wife. Still, the department may have made an example of you for the benefit of the only man who couldn't profit by it."

"Might it not have been, sir, that this suppression was for the good report of the service—as the chief offender was dead?"

"I am glad to hear you say so, General, for it is the argument I have used successfully in behalf of your wife."

"Then you know it all, sir?" said Brant after a gloomy pause.

"All, I think. Come, General, you seemed just now to be uncertain about your enemies. Let me assure you, you need not be so in regard to your friends."

"I dare to hope I have found one, sir," said Brant with almost boyish timidity.

"Oh, not me!" said the President, with a laugh of deprecation. "Some one much more potent."

"May I know his name, Mr. President?"

"No, for it is a woman. You were nearly ruined by one, General. I suppose it's quite right that you should be saved by one. And, of course, irregularly."

"A woman!" echoed Brant.

"Yes; one who was willing to confess herself a worse spy than your wife—a double traitor—to save you! Upon my word, General, I don't know if the department was far wrong; a man with such an alternately unsettling and convincing effect upon a woman's highest political convictions should be under some restraint. Luckily the department knows nothing of it."

"Nor would any one else have known from me," said Brant eagerly. "I trust that she did not think—that you, sir, did not for an instant believe that I"—

"Oh dear, no! Nobody would have believed you! It was her free confidence to me. That was what made the affair so difficult to handle. For even her bringing your dispatch to the division commander looked bad for you; and you know he even doubted its authenticity."

"Does she—does Miss Faulkner know the spy was my wife?" hesitated Brant.

The President twisted himself in his chair, so as to regard Brant more gravely with his deep-set eyes, and then thoughtfully rubbed his leg.

"Don't let us travel out of the record, General," he said after a pause. But as the color surged into Brant's cheek he raised his eyes to the ceiling, and said, in half-humorous recollection,—

"No, I think THAT fact was first gathered from your other friend—Mr. Hooker."

"Hooker!" said Brant, indignantly; "did he come here?"

"Pray don't destroy my faith in Mr. Hooker, General," said the President, in half-weary, half-humorous deprecation. "Don't tell me that any of his inventions are TRUE! Leave me at least that magnificent liar—the one perfectly intelligible witness you have. For from the time that he first appeared here with a grievance and a claim for a commission, he has been an unspeakable joy to me and a convincing testimony to you. Other witnesses have been partisans and prejudiced; Mr. Hooker was frankly true to himself. How else should I have known of the care you took to disguise yourself, save the honor of your uniform, and run the risk of being shot as an unknown spy at your wife's side, except from his magnificent version of HIS part in it? How else should I have known the story of your discovery of the Californian conspiracy, except from his supreme portrayal of it, with himself as the hero? No, you must not forget to thank Mr. Hooker when you meet him. Miss Faulkner is at present more accessible; she is calling on some members of my family in the next room. Shall I leave you with her?"

Brant rose with a pale face and a quickly throbbing heart as the President, glancing at the clock, untwisted himself from the chair, and shook himself out full length, and rose gradually to his feet.

"Your wish for active service is granted, General Brant," he said slowly, "and you will at once rejoin your old division commander, who is now at the head of the Tenth Army Corps. But," he said, after a deliberate pause, "there are certain rules and regulations of your service that even I cannot, with decent respect to your department, override. You will, therefore, understand that you cannot rejoin the army in your former position."

The slight flush that came to Brant's cheek quickly passed. And there was only the unmistakable sparkle of renewed youth in his frank eyes as he said—

"Let me go to the front again, Mr. President, and I care not HOW."

The President smiled, and, laying his heavy hand on Brant's shoulder, pushed him gently towards the door of the inner room.

"I was only about to say," he added, as he opened the door, "that it would be necessary for you to rejoin your promoted commander as a major-general. And," he continued, lifting his voice, as he gently pushed his guest into the room, "he hasn't even thanked me for it, Miss Faulkner!"

The door closed behind him, and he stood for a moment dazed, and still hearing the distant voice of the President, in the room he had just quitted, now welcoming a new visitor. But the room before him, opening into a conservatory, was empty, save for a single figure that turned, half timidly, half mischievously, towards him. The same quick, sympathetic glance was in both their faces; the same timid, happy look in both their eyes. He moved quickly to her side.

"Then you knew that—that—woman was my wife?" he said,

hurriedly, as he grasped her hand.

She cast a half-appealing look at his face—a half-frightened one around the room and at the open door beyond.

"Let us," she said faintly, "go into the conservatory."

*****

It is but a few years ago that the veracious chronicler of these pages moved with a wondering crowd of sightseers in the gardens of the White House. The war cloud had long since lifted and vanished; the Potomac flowed peacefully by and on to where once lay the broad plantation of a great Confederate leader—now a national cemetery that had gathered the soldier dead of both sections side by side in equal rest and honor— and the great goddess once more looked down serenely from the dome of the white Capitol. The chronicler's attention was attracted by an erect, handsome soldierly-looking man, with a beard and moustache slightly streaked with gray, pointing out the various objects of interest to a boy of twelve or fourteen at his side.

"Yes; although, as I told you, this house belongs only to the President of the United States and his family," said the gentleman, smilingly, "in that little conservatory I proposed to your mother."

"Oh! Clarence, how can you!" said the lady, reprovingly, "you know it was LONG after that!"

ABOUT THE AUTHOR

 **Francis Bret Harte** (August 25, 1836–May 6, 1902) was an American author and poet, best remembered for his accounts of pioneering life in California.

Born in Albany, New York, Harte moved to California in 1853, later working there in a number of capacities, including miner, teacher, messenger, and journalist. He spent part of his life in the northern California coast town now known as Arcata, at the time it was just a mining camp on Humboldt Bay.

His first literary efforts, including poetry and prose, appeared in The Californian, an early literary journal edited by Charles Henry Webb. In 1868 he became editor of The Overland Monthly, another new literary magazine, but this one more in tune with the pioneering spirit of excitement in California. His story, "The Luck of Roaring Camp," appeared in the magazine's second edition, propelling Harte to nationwide fame.

As an established literary figure, he was appointed to the position of United States Consul in the town of Krefeld, Germany in 1878 and Glasgow in 1880. In 1885 he settled in London. During the thirty years he spent in Europe, he never abandoned writing, and maintained a prodigious output of stories that retained the freshness of his earlier work. He died in England in 1902.

Choose from Thousands of 1stWorldLibrary Classics By

A. M. Barnard
Ada Leverson
Adolphus William Ward
Aesop
Agatha Christie
Alexander Aaronsohn
Alexander Kielland
Alexandre Dumas
Alfred Gatty
Alfred Ollivant
Alice Duer Miller
Alice Turner Curtis
Alice Dunbar
Allen Chapman
Alleyne Ireland
Ambrose Bierce
Amelia E. Barr
Amory H. Bradford
Andrew Lang
Andrew McFarland Davis
Andy Adams
Angela Brazil
Anna Alice Chapin
Anna Sewell
Annie Besant
Annie Hamilton Donnell
Annie Payson Call
Annie Roe Carr
Annonaymous
Anton Chekhov
Archibald Lee Fletcher
Arnold Bennett
Arthur C. Benson
Arthur Conan Doyle
Arthur M. Winfield
Arthur Ransome
Arthur Schnitzler
Arthur Train
Atticus
B.H. Baden-Powell
B. M. Bower
B. C. Chatterjee
Baroness Emmuska Orczy
Baroness Orczy
Basil King
Bayard Taylor
Ben Macomber
Bertha Muzzy Bower
Bjornstjerne Bjornson

Booth Tarkington
Boyd Cable
Bram Stoker
C. Collodi
C. E. Orr
C. M. Ingleby
Carolyn Wells
Catherine Parr Traill
Charles A. Eastman
Charles Amory Beach
Charles Dickens
Charles Dudley Warner
Charles Farrar Browne
Charles Ives
Charles Kingsley
Charles Klein
Charles Hanson Towne
Charles Lathrop Pack
Charles Romyn Dake
Charles Whibley
Charles Willing Beale
Charlotte M. Braeme
Charlotte M. Yonge
Charlotte Perkins Stetson
Clair W. Hayes
Clarence Day Jr.
Clarence E. Mulford
Clemence Housman
Confucius
Coningsby Dawson
Cornelis DeWitt Wilcox
Cyril Burleigh
D. H. Lawrence
Daniel Defoe
David Garnett
Dinah Craik
Don Carlos Janes
Donald Keyhoe
Dorothy Kilner
Dougan Clark
Douglas Fairbanks
E. Nesbit
E. P. Roe
E. Phillips Oppenheim
E. S. Brooks
Earl Barnes
Edgar Rice Burroughs
Edith Van Dyne
Edith Wharton

Edward Everett Hale
Edward J. O'Biren
Edward S. Ellis
Edwin L. Arnold
Eleanor Atkins
Eleanor Hallowell Abbott
Eliot Gregory
Elizabeth Gaskell
Elizabeth McCracken
Elizabeth Von Arnim
Ellem Key
Emerson Hough
Emilie F. Carlen
Emily Bronte
Emily Dickinson
Enid Bagnold
Enilor Macartney Lane
Erasmus W. Jones
Ernie Howard Pie
Ethel May Dell
Ethel Turner
Ethel Watts Mumford
Eugene Sue
Eugenie Foa
Eugene Wood
Eustace Hale Ball
Evelyn Everett-green
Everard Cotes
F. H. Cheley
F. J. Cross
F. Marion Crawford
Fannie E. Newberry
Federick Austin Ogg
Ferdinand Ossendowski
Fergus Hume
Florence A. Kilpatrick
Fremont B. Deering
Francis Bacon
Francis Darwin
Frances Hodgson Burnett
Frances Parkinson Keyes
Frank Gee Patchin
Frank Harris
Frank Jewett Mather
Frank L. Packard
Frank V. Webster
Frederic Stewart Isham
Frederick Trevor Hill
Frederick Winslow Taylor

Friedrich Kerst	Hayden Carruth	James Branch Cabell
Friedrich Nietzsche	Helent Hunt Jackson	James DeMille
Fyodor Dostoyevsky	Helen Nicolay	James Joyce
G.A. Henty	Hendrik Conscience	James Lane Allen
G.K. Chesterton	Hendy David Thoreau	James Lane Allen
Gabrielle E. Jackson	Henri Barbusse	James Oliver Curwood
Garrett P. Serviss	Henrik Ibsen	James Oppenheim
Gaston Leroux	Henry Adams	James Otis
George A. Warren	Henry Ford	James R. Driscoll
George Ade	Henry Frost	Jane Abbott
Geroge Bernard Shaw	Henry James	Jane Austen
George Cary Eggleston	Henry Jones Ford	Jane L. Stewart
George Durston	Henry Seton Merriman	Janet Aldridge
George Ebers	Henry W Longfellow	Jens Peter Jacobsen
George Eliot	Herbert A. Giles	Jerome K. Jerome
George Gissing	Herbert Carter	Jessie Graham Flower
George MacDonald	Herbert N. Casson	John Buchan
George Meredith	Herman Hesse	John Burroughs
George Orwell	Hildegard G. Frey	John Cournos
George Sylvester Viereck	Homer	John F. Kennedy
George Tucker	Honore De Balzac	John Gay
George W. Cable	Horace B. Day	John Glasworthy
George Wharton James	Horace Walpole	John Habberton
Gertrude Atherton	Horatio Alger Jr.	John Joy Bell
Gordon Casserly	Howard Pyle	John Kendrick Bangs
Grace E. King	Howard R. Garis	John Milton
Grace Gallatin	Hugh Lofting	John Philip Sousa
Grace Greenwood	Hugh Walpole	John Taintor Foote
Grant Allen	Humphry Ward	Jonas Lauritz Idemil Lie
Guillermo A. Sherwell	Ian Maclaren	Jonathan Swift
Gulielma Zollinger	Inez Haynes Gillmore	Joseph A. Altsheler
Gustav Flaubert	Irving Bacheller	Joseph Carey
H. A. Cody	Isabel Cecilia Williams	Joseph Conrad
H. B. Irving	Isabel Hornibrook	Joseph E. Badger Jr
H.C. Bailey	Israel Abrahams	Joseph Hergesheimer
H. G. Wells	Ivan Turgenev	Joseph Jacobs
H. H. Munro	J.G.Austin	Jules Vernes
H. Irving Hancock	J. Henri Fabre	Julian Hawthrone
H. R. Naylor	J. M. Barrie	Julie A Lippmann
H. Rider Haggard	J. M. Walsh	Justin Huntly McCarthy
H. W. C. Davis	J. Macdonald Oxley	Kakuzo Okakura
Haldeman Julius	J. R. Miller	Karle Wilson Baker
Hall Caine	J. S. Fletcher	Kate Chopin
Hamilton Wright Mabie	J. S. Knowles	Kenneth Grahame
Hans Christian Andersen	J. Storer Clouston	Kenneth McGaffey
Harold Avery	J. W. Duffield	Kate Langley Bosher
Harold McGrath	Jack London	Kate Langley Bosher
Harriet Beecher Stowe	Jacob Abbott	Katherine Cecil Thurston
Harry Castlemon	James Allen	Katherine Stokes
Harry Coghill	James Andrews	L. A. Abbot
Harry Houdini	James Baldwin	L. T. Meade

L. Frank Baum	Owen Johnson	Stephen Crane
Latta Griswold	P.G. Wodehouse	Stewart Edward White
Laura Dent Crane	Paul and Mabel Thorne	Stijn Streuvels
Laura Lee Hope	Paul G. Tomlinson	Swami Abhedananda
Laurence Housman	Paul Severing	Swami Parmananda
Lawrence Beasley	Percy Brebner	T. S. Ackland
Leo Tolstoy	Percy Keese Fitzhugh	T. S. Arthur
Leonid Andreyev	Peter B. Kyne	The Princess Der Ling
Lewis Carroll	Plato	Thomas A. Janvier
Lewis Sperry Chafer	Quincy Allen	Thomas A Kempis
Lilian Bell	R. Derby Holmes	Thomas Anderton
Lloyd Osbourne	R. L. Stevenson	Thomas Bailey Aldrich
Louis Hughes	R. S. Ball	Thomas Bulfinch
Louis Joseph Vance	Rabindranath Tagore	Thomas De Quincey
Louis Tracy	Rahul Alvares	Thomas Dixon
Louisa May Alcott	Ralph Bonehill	Thomas H. Huxley
Lucy Fitch Perkins	Ralph Henry Barbour	Thomas Hardy
Lucy Maud Montgomery	Ralph Victor	Thomas More
Luther Benson	Ralph Waldo Emmerson	Thornton W. Burgess
Lydia Miller Middleton	Rene Descartes	U. S. Grant
Lyndon Orr	Ray Cummings	Upton Sinclair
M. Corvus	Rex Beach	Valentine Williams
M. H. Adams	Rex E. Beach	Various Authors
Margaret E. Sangster	Richard Harding Davis	Vaughan Kester
Margret Howth	Richard Jefferies	Victor Appleton
Margaret Vandercook	Richard Le Gallienne	Victor G. Durham
Margaret W. Hungerford	Robert Barr	Victoria Cross
Margret Penrose	Robert Frost	Virginia Woolf
Maria Edgeworth	Robert Gordon Anderson	Wadsworth Camp
Maria Thompson Daviess	Robert L. Drake	Walter Camp
Mariano Azuela	Robert Lansing	Walter Scott
Marion Polk Angellotti	Robert Lynd	Washington Irving
Mark Overton	Robert Michael Ballantyne	Wilbur Lawton
Mark Twain	Robert W. Chambers	Wilkie Collins
Mary Austin	Rosa Nouchette Carey	Willa Cather
Mary Catherine Crowley	Rudyard Kipling	Willard F. Baker
Mary Cole	Saint Augustine	William Dean Howells
Mary Hastings Bradley	Samuel B. Allison	William le Queux
Mary Roberts Rinehart	Samuel Hopkins Adams	W. Makepeace Thackeray
Mary Rowlandson	Sarah Bernhardt	William W. Walter
M. Wollstonecraft Shelley	Sarah C. Hallowell	William Shakespeare
Maud Lindsay	Selma Lagerlof	Winston Churchill
Max Beerbohm	Sherwood Anderson	Yei Theodora Ozaki
Myra Kelly	Sigmund Freud	Yogi Ramacharaka
Nathaniel Hawthrone	Standish O'Grady	Young E. Allison
Nicolo Machiavelli	Stanley Weyman	Zane Grey
O. F. Walton	Stella Benson	
Oscar Wilde	Stella M. Francis